Voices from the Trail of Tears

ALSO BY VICKI ROZEMA

Cherokee Voices:
Early Accounts of Cherokee Life in the East

Footsteps of the Cherokees:
A Guide to the Eastern Homelands of the Cherokee Nation

Voices
from the
Trail of Tears

Edited by Vicki Rozema

BLAIR

*The paper in this book meets the guidelines
for permanence and durability of the
Committee on Production Guidelines for
Book Longevity of the Council on Library Resources.*

Image on front cover—
"Relocation" © Arlene White
(Mohave Tribe)
http://earthrunner.com/4wings

Library of Congress Cataloging-in-Publication Data
Voices from the Trail of Tears / edited by Vicki Rozema.
        p.   cm.—(Real voices, real history series)
Includes bibliographical references and index.
ISBN 978-0-89587-271-5 (alk. paper)
1. Trail of Tears, 1838. 2. Cherokee Indians—Relocation. 3. Cherokee
Indians—History—Sources. 4. Cherokee Indians—Government
relations. 5. Indians, Treatment of—United States—History—19th
century. 6. United States. Act to Provide for an Exchange of Lands with
the Indians Residing in any of the States or Territories, and for Their
Removal West of the River Mississippi. 7. United States—Politics and
government—1815–1861—Sources. 8. Jackson, Andrew, 1767–1845—
Relations with Indians. I. Rozema, Vicki, 1954– II. Series.
E99.C5.V65 2003
973.04'9755—dc21   2002015299

Design by Debra Long Hampton
Composition by The Roberts Group

For my brother and his family, Michael, Donna, Stacy, and Sam Bell

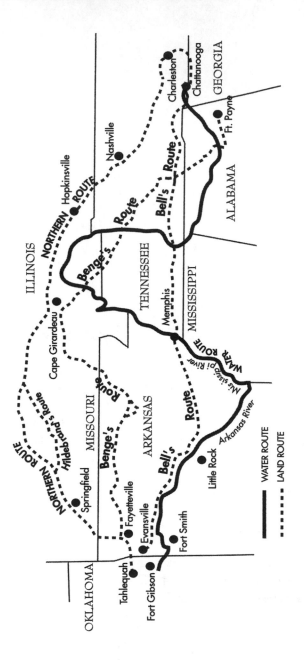

WATER ROUTE
LAND ROUTE

CONTENTS

PREFACE

GROWING UP AROUND CHATTANOOGA, I was vaguely aware that the Trail of Tears passed through this area. Like many Southerners, I heard stories of groups of Indians camped on someone's land or traveling along some old road nearby as they slowly and tragically made their way west. My own family had a story about the removal. My great-great-great-grandmother had avoided the Trail of Tears by marrying a white man, my great-great-great-grandfather. After some research, I now believe they may have met while he was serving in the Alabama militia during the Cherokee Removal.

Although Southerners have heard of the Trail of Tears, most are unaware of the whole story of the removal of the Cherokees or the magnitude of the effort. As a child, I had no idea that the hospital where I was born overlooked the site of a large removal camp located in what is now East Chattanooga. I was unaware that the church I attended in the Brainerd area was located on one of the main removal routes to Ross's Landing. Nor was I aware that one or two thousand Creeks, black slaves, and Cherokees were marched right by the site of the church to the Tennessee River. I lived on Old Harrison Pike for ten years without knowing it was the route used by a detachment of over a thousand Cherokees who crossed the river just north of my home.

Few Chattanoogans are aware that what is now Hamilton County was a bustling center of activity from 1836 to 1838, as United States armed forces, local militia, government emissaries, enrollment agents, physicians, interpreters, supply experts, speculators, and wagon drivers descended on the area in preparation for the huge logistical effort of collecting and feeding the Cherokees prior to transporting them west. And of course, thousands of Cherokees stopped in Chattanooga to enroll for emigration, stopped at the Brainerd Mission on their way to the Red Clay Council meetings, settled here in temporary makeshift quarters after being forced from their homes in Georgia, marched through the area under the threat of artillery to the boats at Ross's Landing, or camped here during the drought-stricken summer of 1838 waiting for Ross's self-removal emigration. These tragic scenes of organized confusion were repeated elsewhere in northern Alabama, northern Georgia, and western North Carolina, but not on as large a scale as they were in Bradley and Hamilton Counties in Tennessee, where the main removal camps and the two main emigrating depots were located.

It wasn't until a few years ago that I began to understand the magnitude and scope of the removal of the southeastern Indians. Thousands of Choctaws, Chickasaws, Creeks, and Seminoles and remnants of other southeastern tribes had undergone forced removal during the 1820s, 1830s, and early 1840s. The story of their emigration is not as well known but is just as tragic. And to the north, the Fox, Sauk, Winnebago, Potawatami, Wyandot, Delaware, Miami, and other tribes were undergoing various forms of removal farther west.

designated officially

During the removal, Cherokees and thousands of other Native Americans were rounded up at gunpoint, separated from their families, forced into stockades, made to travel on foot, by wagon, and by boat to a foreign land, and compelled to start their lives over virtually from scratch. This is a black mark on American history that must be acknowledged. In 1987, the United States Congress recognized the significance of the Cherokee Trail of Tears by designating it a National Historic Trail. Since 1987, the National Park Service, in cooperation with the National Trail of Tears Association and its state chapters, has been seeking to research, document, certify, preserve, and interpret the routes taken by the emigrants and to identify and protect significant sites along the trail. At present, Congress has recognized only those routes taken by emigrating detachments after June 1, 1838—that is, the detachments that left under gunpoint or under John Ross's direction. And congressional legislation thus far has honored only the segments from the main embarkation depots at Guntersville, Chattanooga, and Charleston. But there is an effort under way to ask Congress to officially recognize other sites in other states, including Georgia and North Carolina, that were used during the collection of the Cherokees by including them under the National Historic Trail umbrella.

The exact routes taken by the various detachments are not known at this time. For several years, members of the National Trail of Tears Association and state chapters have been combining their efforts to identify the exact routes and to document other aspects of the Cherokee Removal. During this exacting process, researchers have been able to prove and disprove old stories of where the Cherokees supposedly camped and what roads they used. While significant progress has been made in documenting the Trail of Tears, more research is needed. It may take several more years to finalize the main routes. This unprecedented grass-roots effort to document and certify segments of the trail has led to new efforts to preserve its sites.

As I write, two organizations in Chattanooga—the Chattanooga Regional History Museum and Audubon Acres, also known as the Elise Chapin Wildlife Sanctuary—are undergoing the final steps to be certified as official interpretive sites on the Trail of Tears National Historic Trail. Plans are also being finalized for the new Cherokee Memorial, to be located in Meigs County at Blythe's Ferry, where hundreds of Cherokees camped on the Trail of Tears and thousands crossed the Tennessee River. Efforts are also under way to protect a segment of the Trail of Tears across Moccasin Bend in North Chattanooga as part of the proposed Moccasin Bend National Historic Park. And finally, Vicky Karhu of the Chattanooga Indigenous Resource Center and Library and local members of the Tennessee Trail of Tears Association—especially Doris Tate Trevino, Shirley Lawrence, Carlos Wilson, Bill and Agnes Jones, and, to a lesser degree, myself—have worked with the National Park Service— especially Steve Burns and Aaron Mahr—to identify sites near Ross's Landing and on the north shore so they may be preserved during the impending development of the Chattanooga river front. Recently, their efforts have resulted in planners agreeing to incorporate a new Trail of Tears Memorial at Ross's Landing and agreeing to work with the National Park Service for development of the Trail of Tears National Historic Trail in Chattanooga.

While these recent developments are encouraging, Chattanooga and Meigs County are latecomers to the effort. Other cities and states have already recognized the importance of preserving sites along the Trail of Tears and of developing interpretive centers. These include the Trail of Tears State Park near Cape Girardeau, Missouri; Trail of Tears Commemorative Park in Hopkinsville, Kentucky; Snelson-Brinker House in Crawford County, Missouri; Massey or Maramec Iron Works in Crawford County, Missouri; and New Echota State Park in northern Georgia, to name just a few.

The Cherokee Trail of Tears has become a symbol of the oppression of all Native Americans in the expansion of the United States to the Pacific Ocean. I have compiled this book in the belief that the story can best be told by those who actually participated in this tragic event. *Voices from the Trail of Tears* is a collection of letters, records, and excerpts from journals written by those who witnessed the Cherokee Removal. Though most surviving accounts of the removal were written by white men, I have made an effort to include several letters and accounts written by Cherokees. The selections cover some of the events leading up to removal, the actual removal, and key events that followed.

The first part of the book is a lengthy introduction that gives an overview of the Cherokee Removal. The purpose is to assist in putting the first-person accounts that follow into historical context. I have done minimal editing on the first-person accounts except to insert explanatory remarks in brackets. In researching the Trail of Tears, I have, like researchers before me, encountered confusing and contradictory records and information. I have attempted to resolve these when able. When unable, I have brought the anomalies to the attention of the reader.

During my research, I benefited from the contributions of several individuals and organizations. Special thanks go to my friends in the Tennessee Trail of Tears Association, who shared research material, pointed me toward the location of original and secondary documents, straightened me out on a few points that were confusing or contradictory, or inspired me. These special people include Doris Tate Trevino, Shirley Lawrence, Ken Dubke, and Bill and Agnes Jones. My thanks also go to Aaron Mahr of the Long Distance Trails Group Office of the National Park Service in Santa Fe, New Mexico, who sent me copies of the original journals of Lieutenant Edward Deas and B. B. Cannon; to Vicky Karhu, director of the Chattanooga Indigenous Resource Center and Library; to Jim Ogden, historian at Chickamauga and Chattanooga National Military Park; and to my husband, Edward Rozema, who assisted with typing and indexing.

Permission to use the William Shorey Coodey letter was granted by the staff of the Edward E. Ayer Collection at the Newberry Library in Chicago. Excerpts from the Reverend Daniel S. Butrick's journal are included by permission of the Houghton Library and Harvard University and Dale L. Bishop, executive minister of Wider Church Ministries of the United Church of Christ, the successor of the American Board of Commissioners for Foreign Missions. I express my gratitude to these organizations.

I also express my appreciation to the park rangers and staff at New Echota State Park in Georgia for the use of their library facilities. The librarians and staff at the Chattanooga-Hamilton Country Bicentennial Library and the Lupton Library at the University of Tennessee at Chattanooga, especially Steven Cox, were helpful while I researched this book. The librarians and staff at the Hoskins Library of the University of Tennessee in Knoxville, especially Holly Adams, were also helpful. George Frizzell of the Hunter Library at Western Carolina University has once again proven to be a helpful resource. Finally, I would like to thank all libraries that participate in the interlibrary loan system.

THE BONES OF OUR FATHERS
LIE HERE IN SECURITY,
AND WE CANNOT CONSENT
TO ABANDON THEM
TO BE CRUSHED BENEATH
THE FEET OF STRANGERS.

*Citizens of the
Aquohee District
to the*
Cherokee Phoenix

INTRODUCTION

IN 1828, THE *CHEROKEE PHOENIX* PUBLISHED an editorial titled "Indian's Sorrow" by Elias Boudinot. It told the story of a dinner hosted by General Henry Knox in New York City in 1789. Knox invited a number of Indians to be his guests. One chief went out on the balcony for a few minutes and returned in a melancholy state. General Knox noticed the change of demeanor and asked his guest what was wrong. The elderly man answered,

> I have been looking at your beautiful city—the great water—your fine country—and see how happy you all are. But then I could not help thinking, that this fine country, this great water were once ours. Our ancestors lived here—they enjoyed it as their own in peace—it was the gift of the great spirit to them and their children. At last the white people came in a great canoe. They asked only to let them tie it to a tree, lest the waters should carry it away—we consented. They then said some of their people were sick, and they asked permission to land them and put them under the shade of

the trees. The ice then came, and they could not go away. They then begged a piece of land to build wigwams for the winter—we granted it to them. They then asked for some corn to keep them from starving—we kindly furnished it to them, they promising to go away when the ice was gone. When this happened, we told them they must go away with their big canoe; but they pointed to their big guns round their wigwams, and said they would stay there, and we could not make them go away. Afterwards more came. They brought spirituous and intoxicating liquors with them, of which the Indians became very fond. They persuaded us to sell them some land. Finally they drove us back, from time to time, into the wilderness, far from the water, and the fish, and the oysters—they have destroyed the game—our people have wasted away, and now we live miserable and wretched, while you are enjoying our fine and beautiful country. This makes me sorry brother! and I cannot help it.[1]

By the time Boudinot published the editorial, the Cherokees had established their own representative government, complete with courts and a constitution modeled after that of the United States. Many of the Cherokees could read and write their language using Sequoyah's syllabary or had taken advantage of Christianization programs to receive formal education in English-speaking schools organized by missionaries. Under pressure from the federal government, the Cherokees had transformed themselves into a largely agrarian society. Their former hunting lands having been ceded to the white man, many Cherokees utilized the government's federalization programs, which provided the tools and training to help them adapt to the new economic environment. Under pressure to fit into the white man's world, they had become a society of tavern and turnpike operators, ferrymen, slaveholders, and a few wealthy planters.[2]

felt threatened by Cherokee's economic advancement

By 1828, the Cherokees were staunch allies of the Americans, having assisted them in their negotiations with the Seminoles and other tribes and having provided men to fight under the command of General Andrew Jackson against the Creeks. In spite of the peace that had been in place for nearly three decades, Georgians and some whites in surrounding states felt threatened by the Cherokees' economic advancements and success in formalizing their government. Many state and federal authorities had designs on the Cherokee lands as part of their plans for western expansion. Issues of sovereignty were also a consideration, as state and federal legislators tried to cope with the anomaly of a tribal government with its own laws and courts being located inside state and national boundaries.[3] Many ethnocentric Americans had difficulty distinguishing between their peaceful Cherokee allies and other tribes, or minority groups within tribes. The Cherokees were unfairly tainted by events such as the massacre at Fort Mims in Alabama, during which the Red Sticks, a group of Creek Indians, attacked a small fort and killed several hundred whites.

In 1802, Georgia had made a compact with Congress in which the state agreed to give up its western land claims in exchange for a promise that the federal government would extinguish all remaining Indian titles in Georgia as soon as possible. The pact with Georgia was in conflict with a treaty made a decade earlier in which the federal government had solemnly guaranteed the Cherokees the security of their existing tribal land. The federal government reaffirmed its promise to the Cherokees in 1798.[4] It succeeded in gaining land cessions from Cherokees in other states during the following years, but the Cherokees were still firmly entrenched in Georgia in 1828 and had established their national capital in the state at a place called New Town, or New Echota.

Then, in 1829, gold was discovered near Dahlonega. This was in the heart of the Cherokee Nation, about seventy miles

greed / gold

from New Echota. News of the discovery spread like wildfire and attracted a stampede of prospectors. The greed of the white man to control the gold fields further flamed Georgia's desire to take control of the Cherokee lands.[5] While the discovery of gold has often been given as the primary cause of the expulsion of the Cherokees, it was in reality just one more excuse for the Georgians to remind the federal government of its 1802 promise to take control of the Cherokee lands.

Federal Removal Policy

The concept of Indian removal had its roots in the seventeenth- and eighteenth-century policies of the British and Americans toward Native Americans. Seventeenth-century colonial governments began the practice of restricting eastern Indians from particular areas.[6] The eighteenth century saw the enactment of many land-cession treaties, which began the trend of pushing the Native Americans westward.

Nearly every American president at one time considered the possibility of moving the Indians to areas outside the United States. George Washington envisioned a great boundary line separating whites from Indians. On the advice of a trusted friend, Secretary of War Henry Knox, he settled for a more practical and highly successful program of federalization of the Indians, in which factories or trade houses were established in Indian territory. Agents like Colonel Return J. Meigs were appointed to manage the federal government's interests in Indian affairs, roads were built in Indian territory, and the Indians were taught agricultural, mechanical, and domestic skills to acculturate them to the white man's world. Thomas Jefferson contemplated exchanging Indian lands in the East for vacant lands in the newly acquired Louisiana Territory. James Madison considered similar measures in his effort to pacify the Indians after the War of 1812. John C. Calhoun, secretary of war under James Monroe and a strong advocate of Indian removal, convinced Monroe to adopt a land-swap policy. John Quincy Adams, influenced by the advice of Secretary of War Peter B. Porter, recommended a voluntary exchange of land west of Missouri and Arkansas for Indian territory in the East.[7]

By 1828, Georgia had grown impatient with the federal government's failure to uphold the 1802 agreement. With the election of Andrew Jackson, a known Indian fighter and supporter of states' rights, the Georgians were encouraged to take matters into their own hands. Within a month of Jackson's election, Georgia passed the first of several laws designed to attack the sovereignty of the Cherokee Nation within its borders. The new law was to become effective June 1, 1830. It annexed to Georgia all the lands of the Cherokees within the state, made null and void the laws and customs established by the Cherokees, and forbade any person of Indian blood to act as a witness in a suit in which a white man was the defendant.

The debate reached a crescendo in 1829 and 1830, when an Indian removal bill was brought before Congress. The bill, encouraged by President Jackson and his supporters, was based on a plan he had introduced in his negotiations with the Cherokees in 1817. However, the new plan would apply to all Indian tribes. For the first step, the Indians would receive permanent title to tracts of land west of the Mississippi River in exchange for their eastern land. The new lands would lie outside the boundaries of all states in the union, which would eliminate the problem of tribal governments existing within sovereign states. Secondly, individual allotments of land would be given to those Indians desiring to remain in the East who agreed to become citizens of the states in which they resided. The president thought that only a few of the most educated and land-wealthy mixed-bloods would choose to remain in the East. They would need to acknowledge the superiority of state laws over tribal laws. Jackson believed this measure would eventually end the need for complex treaty making. The final goals of the removal bill were to open vast areas of land to white settlement in the near West and to benefit the Indians by giving them lands of their own away from the white man.[8]

Jackson's policies on Indian removal faced stiff criticism from different sources. Jeremiah Evarts, a Congregationalist leader and corresponding secretary of the American Board of Commissioners for Foreign Missions, denounced Indian removal as an attempt "to drive the Indians, by force, from their country." Evarts, using the pseudonym William Penn, wrote a number of essays criticizing the removal practice that were widely circulated in the *National Intelligencer* and reprinted in the *Cherokee Phoenix*. These essays did much to arouse the sympathy of the American public for the Cherokees.[9]

Other critics of the Indian Removal Act, such as Senator Theodore Frelinghuysen of New Jersey, attacked Jackson's policy on moral grounds. Congressman William W. Ellsworth of Connecticut expressed his doubts about the benevolent intentions of the removal supporters in a speech to the House of Representatives in May 1830: "I have no doubt that mercenary motives, in some of the southern and south-western portions of the country have had, and still have, an important influence upon this measure." Other anti-removal spokesmen included Peleg Sprague of Maine, who argued that Jackson would use any funds appropriated for the removal to pay for guns and bayonets, Asher Robbins of Rhode Island, Daniel Webster, the great orator and senator from Massachusetts, and the politically astute Henry Clay of Kentucky. Some of Jackson's opponents, like Clay, had previously argued that Indians were inferior to whites and would not be missed should they disappear. Clay changed his position when Indian removal became associated with Jackson's party in the minds of the public.[10]

When the removal bill went before the House for a vote, Congressman David Crockett of Tennessee voted against it. His opposition to the bill and to other Jackson policies cost him reelection to Congress the following year. After the debates in Congress on the removal bill—the official record of which does not show a speech given by Crockett—a book was published that included a summary of a speech purported to be one he had given or planned to give to Congress. The author reported Crockett as having told Congress he "did not know whether a man within 500 miles of his residence would give a similar vote; but he knew, at the same time, that he should give that vote with a clear conscience. . . . He had always viewed the native Indian tribes of this country as a sovereign people. He believed they had been recognized as such from the very foundation of this government, and the United States were bound by treaty to protect them; it was their duty to do so." Crockett had also received a delegation of Cherokees visiting Washington and introduced them to some of the Kentucky congressmen. John Ridge met the powerful Henry Clay and was persuaded that the newfound friendship with Clay and the Whigs would be enough to stop the bill from passing.[11]

On May 28, 1830, Congress passed the Indian Removal Act. It provided for the exchange of Indian lands in any state or territory of the United States for lands west of the Mississippi River and for the removal of the Indians to those lands. Congress thus gave its approval to Jackson's removal scheme. Under Jackson, War Department officials negotiated nearly seventy Indian treaties that were ratified by the Senate—a record unmatched by any other administration. The overwhelming majority of them involved land cessions. To obtain these treaties, the War Department ignored tribal sovereignty by encouraging American treaty commissioners to select the individual leaders or parts of a tribe with whom they would negotiate. In the case of the Cherokees, commissioners exploited the growing tribal divisions among the Cherokees and encouraged a minority group to sign the Treaty of New Echota, which called for the emigration of the entire nation.[12]

By the end of Jackson's term in January 1837, his administration had moved forty-six thousand Indians from their lands and had negotiated treaties yet to be carried out providing for the removal of still more. "Old Hickory," as Jackson was fondly called by his supporters, played a major role in the separation of eastern Indians from their homelands.[13]

Some historians and writers have equated Jackson's removal policy with Adolph Hitler's Final Solution or called it genocide.[14] Not only did he encourage the geographical separation of Indians and whites, but thousands of Native Americans perished in the process. Most of these deaths occurred from disease, rather than violence. Other historians note that Jackson offered to pay the Indians for their land and suggest that his main ambition was to promote American expansion while trying to preserve Indian culture. On one hand, he could be a ruthless opponent in battle against Indians. On the other hand, he exhibited paternalistic tendencies in his dealings with the Indians as territorial governor of Florida. He also sanctioned Indian-white marriages and had full-blooded Indians as friends. Jackson adopted a Creek Indian orphan named Lincoyer and raised him at the Hermitage, his home near Nashville.[15] He was not an admirer of the ways of Indian life, but he did not advocate the mass extinction of Indians. Jackson was a follower of the Republican doctrine of state sovereignty and believed the federal government should have limited powers. If individual states wanted to expel the Indians, he would not stop what he believed to be their right but would instead help them establish the superiority of their laws over tribal laws and help secure westward expansion in the process. Indians wishing to remain in the East could do so and would even receive land allotments, but they must become citizens of the states where they resided.[16]

Georgia v. the Cherokees

In June 1830, within days of the passage of the federal removal bill, Governor George R. Gilmer of Georgia issued a proclamation prohibiting the Indians from taking any more gold from their lands. Gilmer claimed that Georgia owned title to the Cherokee lands, as well as all mineral rights. He essentially accused the Cherokees of stealing from the citizens of Georgia by mining their own property. The governor's proclamation was published in the *Cherokee Phoenix*.[17]

Georgia also passed laws prohibiting the National Council from meeting within the state and calling for the abolishment of the Cherokee constitution. In 1831, surveyors entered the Cherokee Nation and began dividing the six thousand square miles of Cherokee lands in Georgia into either 160-acre land lots or 40-acre gold lots, which were to be distributed to Georgia citizens in a land lottery the following year. In the land lottery, the homes of both poor and prosperous Cherokees were given away to lucky winners, who moved in quickly and kicked out the Cherokees. Even prominent Cherokees like John Ross and Joseph Vann were forced from their homes. However, the property belonging to those favoring removal was temporarily withdrawn from the lottery or declared exempt from immediate confiscation. In 1834, Governor Wilson Lumpkin instructed the federal enrolling officer to "assure Boudinot, Ridge, and their friends of state protection under any circumstances."[18]

In 1832, Cherokee Council meetings were relocated from Georgia to the Red Clay Council Grounds in Tennessee. Many Cherokees also moved their homes from Georgia to Tennessee, to the disappointment of many people of the latter state. John Ross made his home at Red Hill, near the council grounds and nearer to his brother Lewis Ross, a successful businessman living in Charleston, Tennessee. Joseph Vann, or "Rich Joe," had already established a farm on the Tennessee River. When he lost his plantation in Georgia, he moved to his home on the Tennessee.

In December 1830, Moravian, Congregationalist, Baptist, and Presbyterian missionaries met at New Echota and crafted a resolution supporting the Cherokees. The Methodists had already drawn up a similar memorial. The resolutions were published in the *Missionary Herald*. When news leaked out in Georgia, a law was passed prohibiting white men from remaining in Cherokee lands within the state. Not to be intimidated, the missionaries ignored the law. On March 12, 1831, the first of several arrests of missionaries began. After being released on the basis that they were acting as agents of the federal government in their positions as postmasters and because they were handling federal funds to educate and civilize the Indians, several were rearrested. At a hearing before the Georgia Supreme Court, nine of the missionaries relented to the state's will and were released. However, two missionaries, Elizur Butler and Samuel Worcester, refused to submit to the sovereignty of Georgia over the Cherokees and were sentenced to four years of hard labor. The situation of the missionaries elicited great sympathy for the Cherokee cause. The missionaries and the Cherokees were encouraged to take the case before the United States Supreme Court.[19]

In early 1832, John Ridge and Elias Boudinot were in Washington when news arrived of the Supreme Court's decision in the case of *Worcester v. Georgia*. The decision was in favor of the missionaries and the Cherokees. It declared the Cherokee Nation to be sovereign and the act of Georgia under which the missionaries were arrested to be null and void.[20] It appeared to be a great victory for the Cherokee cause.

But the elation that John Ridge felt upon hearing the news didn't last long. He immediately asked for and received an audience with President Jackson to see what his intentions were in respect to freeing the missionaries and protecting the

Cherokees from the Georgians. Jackson made it clear he would not do anything to enforce the court's ruling. Instead, he pleaded with Ridge to go home and advise his people that their only hope was to abandon their country and move west. Jackson later wrote of this meeting with Ridge and said that Ridge expressed despair. A member of Jackson's Kitchen Cabinet, Amos Kendall, later wrote that this was the moment John Ridge reversed his position on removal. However, Ridge wrote to Stand Watie about the Supreme Court decision, "I can readily perceive and congratulate them upon the momentous event. . . . But Sir, the Chicken Snake General Jackson has time to crawl and hide in the luxuriant grass of his nefarious hypocrisy until his responsibility is fastened upon by an execution of the Supreme Court at their next session. Then we shall see how strong the links are to the chain that connect the states to the Federal Union."[21]

Before Ridge and the delegation visiting Washington returned to Cherokee country, rumors began circulating that the delegation was considering removal because of Jackson's intransigence. The delegation denied it had changed positions. Then, in early May, Ridge received a letter from David Greene of the American Board of Commissioners for Foreign Missions advising him that most political groups in Washington now felt the situation was hopeless. The Supreme Court decision was useless without force to back it up. He advised Ridge to enter into a treaty.[22]

A Nation Divided

In 1832, a deep rift developed in the Cherokee political leadership on the issue of removal. Those favoring negotiations for a fair removal treaty became known as the Treaty Party. Prominent supporters of negotiating for removal included Major Ridge and his son John; John Adair Bell; William Hicks;

Elias Boudinot; Stand Watie, Boudinot's brother; and Andrew Ross, John Ross's brother. Many of these men had fought hard to preserve Cherokee lands in the East and were staunch patriots. Major Ridge had ridden throughout the land speaking against removal. His son John recorded a speech his father made at Turkeytown in Alabama in February 1829: "If the country, to which we are directed to go is desirable and well watered, why is it so long a wilderness and a waste, and uninhabited by respectable white people, whose enterprise ere this would have induced them to monopolize it from the poor and unfortunate of their fellow citizens as they have hitherto done? From correct information we have formed a bad opinion of the western country beyond the Mississippi. But if report was favorable to the fertility of the soil, if the running streams were as transparent as crystal, and silver fish abounded in their element in profusion, we should still adhere to the purpose of spending the remnant of our lives on the soil that gave us birth, and is rendered dear from the nourishment we received from its bosom."[23]

As Boudinot's views began to change in favor of removal, he felt the Cherokee people had a right to read arguments on both sides of the issue. However, the Cherokee government prohibited him from publishing his views on removal in the *Cherokee Phoenix*. Boudinot resigned as editor in August 1832. John Ross's brother-in-law, Elijah Hicks, replaced Boudinot as editor. In 1835, Ross's plan to move the *Phoenix*'s printing press to Red Clay for protection was thwarted when the Georgia Guard confiscated the press, type, paper, and books.[24]

Between 1832 and 1835, the rift between the National Party—as the John Ross faction came to be called—and the Treaty Party—as the Ridge faction was called—widened to the point of violence. In August 1834, John Walker, Jr., was shot as he was returning home from a council at Red Clay, supposedly because of his opinions in favor of removal. The two parties held separate meetings with federal authorities and sent separate emissaries to Washington. At one point, Andrew Ross and three of his followers signed a treaty containing terms of removal that even his fellow Treaty Party members objected to. That treaty was never ratified by the Senate.[25]

In the fall of 1834, the two parties held separate councils. At the Treaty Party council at Running Waters, the members drew up a resolution explaining their position on removal. It read, in part, "[The Treaty Party delegates] express . . . the sorrowful conviction that it is impossible for them, in the present state of things, to retain their national existence, and to live in peace and comfort in their native region. They therefore have turned their eyes to the country west of the Mississippi, to which a considerable portion of their tribe have already emigrated; and they express the opinion that they are reduced to the alternative of following them to that region, or of sinking into a condition but little, if at all, better than slavery."[26]

The War Department decided to snub the Ross faction for the time being and to deal primarily with the Treaty Party. It sent an emissary, a former parson from New York, John F. Schermerhorn, to negotiate with the Ridge faction. But the federal government couldn't shake Ross's persistent appeals for discussion, and Ross was kept in the negotiations for most of 1835. In October, a council was held at Red Clay at which Schermerhorn and both parties were present. In a brief moment of unity, both parties rejected an earlier treaty sponsored by Ridge. Then Schermerhorn called for a new council to be held in New Echota in December. Both Boudinot and John Ridge warned Schermerhorn that few, if any, Cherokees would attend, but he persisted. In November, he published a notice of the meeting, supposedly printed on the confiscated *Phoenix* press.[27]

Shortly after the October council, Ross was arrested at his home in Red Hill, Tennessee. The Georgia Guard took possession of his private papers and the records of the council. John Howard Payne, author of "Home Sweet Home," was visiting

Ross at his home and was also arrested. They were taken to Spring Place, where they were held in chains. Ross was imprisoned for twelve days, then released without apology or explanation. Payne was held for thirteen days, then ordered out of Cherokee country.[28]

Three hundred to four hundred Cherokees showed up for the meeting at New Echota. A committee of twenty men did most of the work of negotiating with Schermerhorn on the terms of a treaty. On December 29, 1835, those twenty men signed or made their marks on the fateful Treaty of New Echota, which signed away the Cherokee lands in the East in return for $5 million and the cost of emigration. The signers of the treaty included Major Ridge, Elias Boudinot, John Gunter, Andrew Ross, and John Adair Bell, a friend of John Ridge's and son of a prominent Cherokee family. John Ridge and Stand Watie signed the treaty on March 1. Endorsed in the Senate by a margin of one vote, it was ratified by Congress on May 23, 1836.[29]

The terms of the 1835 treaty mandated that within two years of its ratification, the Cherokee Nation must give up its lands in Alabama, Georgia, North Carolina, and Tennessee and emigrate to territory set aside for it in what is now Oklahoma. However, the treaty also stated that individuals and families that were averse to removal could become citizens of the states where they resided, with the exception of Georgia, and would become subject to the laws of those states. They would be allotted 160 acres of land.[30]

Preparing for Removal

Shortly after the Treaty of New Echota was ratified, government agents began assessing the Cherokee lands for improvements. They were charged with assigning cash values to all improvements made by the Cherokees. The evaluations were completed in 1837.[31]

General John E. Wool was sent with American troops to the Cherokee Nation. His orders were to police the country and disarm the Cherokees. Local and federal officials were concerned there might be armed resistance before the removal could be carried out.[32]

Ross, however, managed to keep everyone relatively calm as he tried to have the treaty overturned. He and the national delegates sent a protest to Congress containing signatures representing nearly sixteen thousand Cherokees. Councils were held denouncing the methods used to secure the treaty and declaring it null and void. General Wool forwarded the protests to Washington, explaining, "It is, however, vain to talk to a people almost universally opposed to the treaty and who maintain that they never made such a treaty. So determined are they in their opposition that not one of all those who were present and voted at the council held but a day or two since, however poor or destitute, would either receive rations or clothing from the United States lest they might compromise themselves in regard to the treaty. . . . Many have said they will die before they will leave the country."[33]

Jackson rebuked General Wool for forwarding the protests, declaring them disrespectful to the president, the Senate, and the American people. But Major W. M. Davis, appointed to enroll the Cherokees for removal and to appraise their property, supported General Wool's position and forwarded a similar letter.[34] The enrollment for removal was supposed to be voluntary, and neither Wool nor Davis desired a violent confrontation with the Cherokees based on an invalid treaty.

The Cherokee census conducted in 1835 counted over 16,500 tribal members in the East. Another 5,000 Cherokees already resided west of the Mississippi, most of whom had emigrated during the preceding two decades.[35]

The removal of over 16,000 Cherokees would be a massive undertaking, but the War Department and the Bureau of Indian

Affairs had acquired a good deal of experience moving Indians and were prepared for this latest effort. They immediately began the enrollment process with hopes that the first detachment would leave before the end of 1836.

The 1837 Emigrations

The first detachment of Cherokees departed around January 1, 1837. The group consisted of six hundred members of the Treaty Party, mostly middle-class and upper-middle-class families who took their slaves, horses, and droves of oxen. They made their own plans and followed a land route through Tennessee, Kentucky, Illinois, Missouri, and Arkansas. No deaths were reported in this group.[36]

Major Ridge, wife Susanna, son Walter, granddaughter Clarinda, and eighteen slaves departed Ross's Landing on March 3, 1837, for their new homes in the West. The detachment consisted of 466 emigrants under the direction of Dr. John S. Young. It was a government-run operation. The detachment traveled by water aboard steamboats hauling eleven flatboats and by train. Several physicians were hired, including Dr. Samuel M. Doak and Dr. Clark C. Lillybridge. Four deaths were reported on this journey, although a number of emigrants suffered from illness, including Major Ridge. The detachment arrived at its destination in late March.[37]

John Ridge, Elias Boudinot, and their families traveled west via horse and carriage. When they stopped in Nashville to have their horses shod, Ridge took the opportunity to visit the aging Andrew Jackson, who was blind in one eye, almost deaf, and in declining health. After seven weeks of travel, they arrived at their destination in late November 1837. John Ridge settled into his new home quickly and started stocking his store in anticipation of the arrival of the fifteen thousand additional Cherokees he was sure would come eventually.[38]

tried to lobby

In the meantime, John Ross continued to try to rouse support in Washington to have the treaty nullified and the emigration stopped. His efforts were in vain. He next tried to write new treaties that would allow all the Cherokees to declare themselves citizens so they could stay, and that would also reimburse them for the lands they were forfeiting. He lobbied the new president, Martin Van Buren, a Jackson crony, without success. At one point, Van Buren momentarily agreed to postpone the deadline for removal until 1840, but that agreement was quickly overturned.[39]

In North Carolina, William Holland Thomas, the white agent and leader of the Qualla Indians, called together all the Cherokees in his area for a meeting. He asked if they wanted to remain in their homeland or emigrate west. Everyone voted to remain. Thomas had recently been to Washington to negotiate with authorities over the legal status of the Qualla Indians and had already secured promises that they could stay. However, to further solidify their position, Thomas began pressuring state and local officials to recognize their legal status as citizens of North Carolina. Preliminary state approval was granted in September 1837 but was not finalized.[40] The Qualla Indians would watch their fellow Cherokees being rounded up at gunpoint, all the while fearing that they might also be included.

Collection   *deadline 5-23-1838*

By the time May 23, 1838, the deadline for removal, arrived, only a few detachments totaling approximately two thousand Cherokees had enrolled and left for the West. These were mostly Treaty Party supporters.

General Winfield Scott had replaced Colonel William Lindsay, who had temporarily replaced General Wool after complaints from the Georgians and others that Wool was growing soft toward the Cherokees. Scott and Wool had both warned the Cherokees on several occasions that they should prepare for removal. Once the deadline was reached, Scott immediately began issuing orders for the removal to begin: "The commanding officer at every fort & open station will first cause to be surrounded and brought in as many Indians, the nearest to his fort or station, as he may think he can secure at once, & repeat the operation until he shall have made as many prisoners as he is able to subsist and send off, under a proper escort, to the most convenient of the emigrating depots, the Cherokee Agency, Ross Landing, and Gunter's Landing.

"These operations will be again and again repeated under the order of the commanders of the respective districts, until the whole of the Indians shall have been collected for emigration."[41]

General Scott had approximately two thousand United States soldiers in his command during the Cherokee Removal. Two regiments of artillery—the Second and Third Regiments—were stationed at Ross's Landing.[42] Kept under guard by large numbers of mounted soldiers and local militia, the Cherokees were forced to march from one temporary camp to the next as they made their way to the emigration depots.

The artillery and armed guards notwithstanding, Scott issued orders that the collection and removal should be carried out in as humane a manner as possible. Soldiers were to refrain from unnecessary acts of violence or harshness. Cherokees too sick to travel were to be left at the three main emigrating depots—Gunter's Landing, Ross's Landing, and Fort Cass in Charleston—and cared for by a family member until they were well enough to travel. The roundup began in Georgia and was continued a few days later in North Carolina, Tennessee, and Alabama.[43]

James Mooney, who lived with the Cherokees for three years in the late nineteenth century, spoke with members of the tribe who had experienced the collection. He provided the following description, given from the Cherokee viewpoint:

"Under Scott's orders the troops were disposed at various points throughout the Cherokee country, where stockade forts were erected for gathering in and holding the Indians preparatory to removal. From these, squads of troops were sent to search out with rifle and bayonet every small cabin hidden away in the coves or by the sides of mountain streams, to seize and bring in as prisoners all the occupants, however or wherever they might be found. Families at dinner were startled by the sudden gleam of bayonets in the doorway and rose up to be driven with blows and oaths along the weary miles of trail that led to the stockade. Men were seized in their fields or going along the road, women were taken from their wheels and children from their play."[44]

William J. Cotter, who was fourteen and living in Georgia at the time, experienced the Cherokee Removal firsthand when his father was hired to furnish supplies for one of the Georgia posts. Cotter and his father made $5.00 a day. On one day, they made $13.00. They worked from early morning until late at night. Years later, William J. Cotter described the experience in his autobiography:

> The men [soldiers] handled them gently, but picked them up in the road, in the field, anywhere they found them, part of a family at a time, and carried them to the post. Everything in their homes was left only for a day or two and then hauled to the post. When a hundred or more families had been collected, they were marched to Ross's Landing (now Chattanooga). It was a mournful sight to all who witnessed it—old men and women with gray hairs walking with the sad company. Provisions were made for those to ride who could not walk.
>
> I had a part in all this tragic scene. Col. W. J. Howard, the quartermaster, boarded with us and kept his office in the Harlan house. There were no army wagons and teams, and

he hired what he needed and gave father the privilege of furnishing some of the supplies for the post. Horses and oxen did most of the work. We had a yoke, strong and true, and they walked nearly as fast as horses. I was the driver, and I hauled the first corn for their horses and perhaps the last. . . . In hauling the stuff from the cabins a file of six or more men went with me as a guard. They forced open the doors and put the poor, meager household effects into the wagons, sometimes the stuff of two or three families at one load.[45]

As small groups of Cherokees were rounded up, they were brought to stockade areas for temporary holding until they could be moved to the main emigration depots.[46] Some of these groups were moved along quickly. Others were held longer and moved in groups of several hundred to a thousand to the emigration depots.

A map drawn by Lieutenant E. D. Keyes illustrating General Scott's operations shows forts scattered across the region. Fort Payne, Fort Lovell, and Fort Likens were located in northeastern Alabama. In Tennessee, forts were located at or near Red Clay, Cleveland, and Ross's Landing. Also in Tennessee were Fort Morrow, on the road from Spring Place to the Cherokee Agency at Charleston, and Fort Cass, located at that same agency. In North Carolina, the military forts included Fort Lindsay, near the eastern end of what is now Fontana Lake, Fort Butler near Murphy, Fort Hembree near Hayesville, Fort Montgomery at Cheowee, Fort Delaney on the Valley River at what is now Andrews, and Camp Scott at the mouth of the Nantahala River. At least thirteen forts were scattered across northwestern Georgia, including Fort Wool at New Echota, Fort Hoskins at Spring Place, and forts at Rome, Dahlonega, and Cedartown.[47]

Although most of these forts were temporary, the job of supplying and maintaining them was complex and expensive for the government. William A. Lenoir was serving as acting assistant quartermaster at Gunter's Landing in March when he was ordered to send all the "subsistence stores remaining at the Landing [Gunter's Landing]" to a new post being established at Cedar Bluff, Alabama. A company of infantry would arrive April 7, 1838, at the new post, which would be named Fort Lovell. Approximately sixty-four soldiers staffed the fort initially. In the middle of June, the number increased to seventy-two. There were also three women at the fort, who were probably hired as cooks or laundresses. They may have been wives of the soldiers or local women. Lenoir kept detailed records of supplies that were brought into the post, issued to the Cherokees and soldiers, consumed, left over, sold at auction when the fort was abandoned, and shipped off to other locations. These records provide clues to what life was like for both soldiers and Cherokees at the hastily constructed, temporary forts.

Early expenses included $64.50 to hire men to haul timber for the construction of Fort Lovell and another $43.50 to transport baggage and supplies from Gunter's Landing for the Alabama Volunteers. The timber used to construct the stockade may have been hauled directly behind teams of oxen without the use of wagons or sleds. In all, over $325.00 was spent in the first month to hire at least nine men to haul provisions and to lease their teams of oxen and horses. Also during the first month of operations, 58 barrels of flour (weighing approximately 196 pounds each), 4,000 pounds of bacon, six bushels of salt, 547 pounds of soap, 1236½ pounds of sugar, 827 pounds of coffee, 156 pounds of rice, 240 pounds of candles, and 18 gallons of vinegar were purchased. During the same period, nine barrels and 140 pounds of flour, 1,385 pounds of bacon, one bushel and 12 quarts of salt, 64 pounds and five ounces of soap, 134 pounds and 10 ounces of sugar, 68 pounds and 13 ounces of coffee, all of the rice, 26 pounds and 11 ounces of candles, and 16 gallons and three quarts of vinegar were either issued to the troops or wasted.

Other purchases for the fort during the three months it was in operation included sandpaper, boxes of wafers, sealing wax, 100 quills, bottles of ink, paper, a desk, a table, a ruler, six chairs, one adze, hatchets, spades, axes, six augers, blankets, bridles, chisels, wedges, drawing knives, harnesses, hammers, hinges, files, 489 pounds of iron, one side of leather, three kinds of locks, 325 pounds of nails, 4,495 feet of wooden planks, saddles, saws, steel yards (for measuring weight), two walled tents with flies, 12 common tents, 12 camp kettles, 24 mess pans, and a grindstone. The two walled tents were probably for the use of the four officers, while the common tents were probably the quarters for the enlisted men, who slept six per tent. Captain Thomas B. Watts also acquired a drum and a fife for his men. Considering all the food, soap, and musical instruments purchased for the fort, the men must have been well fed, clean, and entertained.

When the collection of the Cherokees began in early June, Lenoir received instructions from Lieutenant Charles Hoskins that he should issue one pound of flour or, if they preferred, one pint of corn and one half-pound of bacon per day "to each Indian, man, woman, or child" brought into Fort Lovell. For the quarter ending June 30, 1838, some 95 bushels of corn and 1,280 bundles of fodder were issued for the Cherokees' horses. For the same period, 84½ bushels of corn and 2,352 bundles of fodder were issued for the soldiers' horses.

Lenoir kept records of rations issued to the Cherokees. The first were distributed on June 5 and the last on June 27. These records provide clues as to approximately how many Cherokees passed through Fort Lovell on their way to Gunter's Landing or the camps near Fort Payne. It appears that approximately 807 Cherokees were taken to Fort Lovell and then held for up to nine days before being sent on. At one point, 224 Indians were held in the fort. The last detachment of Cherokees appears to have left Fort Lovell on June 30.

On July 3, Lenoir received a communication from Lieutenant Hoskins stating that the forts used for collection of the Cherokees in Alabama were to be abandoned immediately, with the exception of Fort Payne. Lenoir left Fort Lovell that day for Fort Payne. Captain Watts and his company, who had been stationed at Fort Lovell, departed on July 3 for Gunter's Landing. Lenoir left the subsistence stores in the hands of "Esquire Nichols in whom I have every confidence." He had to return briefly to Fort Lovell to wrap things up. The unused stores of flour and bacon were sent to the Indian agent at Rawlingsville, three miles north of Fort Payne, possibly for the use of the Cherokees in the nearby camp. At the end of July, Lenoir auctioned off all the hardware to local citizens.[48]

Scott and his officers filed frequent reports on how the roundup and emigration were progressing. All in all, matters proceeded quickly and with few incidents of resistance from the Cherokees.

Nathaniel Smith, the superintendent of Cherokee Removal, was charged with keeping records of emigrating Cherokees, making provisions for supplies in the camps and on the emigration routes, providing transportation westward, and reporting the progress to his superior, C. A. Harris, commissioner of Indian Affairs. On June 1, 1838, Harris passed on information he had received from Scott on the progress of the roundup. At the end of the excerpt below, he refers to two detachments totaling 716 Cherokees who were sent voluntarily in October 1837 and April 1838. As of June 1, when this letter was written, no detachments of forced emigrants had left the depots. "On the 30th ult. [ultimo, i.e. the previous month, May] I received a letter from Genl. Scott, who states the business of collecting the Cherokees in the limits of Georgia is going on finely. More than two thirds are before this time collected and on their route to the Depots established for their reception. I shall on Monday next start a party of 1000 or more by water, and after that every ten days will be prepared to send off that number until all are removed. After the Third party, unless otherwise instructed, I will on account of their health send them up the Missouri to Boonesville [Missouri]. . . . It is worthy of remark that I have sent 716 by water and but two of them died, both children, whereas out of the party of 365 who went last fall by land Sixteen died, five adults and Eleven children."[49]

By June 6, General Scott had nearly wrapped up the collection of Indians in Georgia. This included approximately five hundred Creeks who had fled there a year or two earlier to escape the more violent Creek Removal. Scott reported to Nathaniel Smith that "all the Georgia Indians, except a few families and fugitives in the mountains, will, I think, be in our hands by the 10th instant, and we shall begin, vigorously, to make collections in the other three States on the 12th instant. You, will, therefore, have your hands full in this and the ensuing month, as well as at present."[50]

Forced Emigrations Commence @ gunpoint

On June 6, Nathaniel Smith sent off the first detachment of Cherokees at gunpoint. At Ross's Landing, eight hundred Cherokees and their slaves, mostly from Georgia, were loaded on to flatboats pulled by a steamboat. Lieutenant Edward Deas, a very capable soldier with previous experience leading detachments of emigrating Creeks and Cherokees, was assigned to the boats.[51] Excerpts from his journal of the voyage are provided in the chapter titled "Under Weigh at Daylight."

After the first groups of Cherokees were sent off, John Ross and members of the Cherokee Council finally accepted their fate. Cherokee runners were sent out to ask those hiding in the mountains to join the rest of the nation and not be left behind. The army was pleased that the Reverend Jesse Bushyhead agreed to be one of the runners.[52]

Scott expanded the boundaries of the main camps as new emigrants were brought in. The largest camp was at Fort Cass, located at the Cherokee Agency in Charleston, Tennessee. It was eventually expanded to an area twelve miles long by four miles wide.[53]

Scott painted a bright picture of the collection in this letter to Secretary of War Joel R. Poinsett, dated June 26:

> The collection of the Indians in No. Carolina, Tennessee & Alabama, goes on well, & may almost be considered as almost completed. Late reports from Brigadier General Eustis and Colonel Lindsay are to that effect. The few families & individuals in the No. Carolina & other mountains, will, I have no doubt, soon be induced to come in by the Indian runners sent or to be sent out for the purpose. Mr. Bushyhead one of the runners alluded to, had not reached Valley river at the date of Brig. Genl. Eustis's last note. . . .
>
> For the accommodation of the Indians with wood, shade & good water, I have greatly extended the limits of this emigrating depot. It is now about three miles & a half long & three in width. Families & individuals, with very few exceptions, have become cheerful. I have ordered all, who require it, to be vaccinated. The operation has commenced, & the supplies of every sort are abundant.[54]

Two more large detachments of Cherokees were sent off June 15 and June 17 from Ross's Landing. One of the parties, numbering just under nine hundred people, was under the command of Lieutenant R. H. K. Whitely. The Cherokees were crowded on to flatboats and hauled by a circuitous river route using various steamboats—the *George Guess*, the *Smelter*, and the *Tecumseh*. They arrived in Indian territory in early August. The last party to leave from Ross's Landing before emigration was stopped for the summer was under the command of Lieutenant

G. S. Drane. On June 17, his detachment was marched from Ross's Landing to Waterloo, Alabama, where it boarded boats for the remainder of the trip west.[55] More information on the Whitely and Drane detachments may be found in the chapter titled "Feelings of Discontent."

On June 19, Scott ordered the postponement of emigration until cooler, wetter, healthier weather. Ross and other leading Cherokees approached Scott with the idea of allowing the Cherokees to organize their own removal.[56]

While the emigration was put on hold pending a final agreement on self-removal, which was to commence by September 1, Cherokees continued to be brought in. In a letter dated June 28, 1838, L. B. Webster described his experience in bringing Cherokees from North Carolina to Fort Cass: "I left Fort Butler on the 19th in charge of 800 Cherokees. I had not an officer along to assist me, and only my own company as a guard. Of course I have as much to do as I could attend to. But I experienced no difficulty in getting them along, other than what arose from fatigue, and this toughness of the roads over the mountains; which are the worst I ever saw. I arrived with about one hundred more than what I started with. Many having joined me on the march. We were eight days in making the journey (80 miles), and it was pitiful to behold the women & children, who suffered exceedingly—as they were all obliged to walk, with the exception of the sick."[57]

Sickness in the Camps

When emigration was halted, there remained approximately thirteen thousand Cherokees to be sent west. They were collected in multiple camps spread out over a large area in Tennessee and Alabama, each located near water and guarded by soldiers. There were at least two large camps in the Chattanooga area. Other camps were located near Fort Payne, Red

Clay, Cleveland, Charleston, and on the roads between those towns and Charleston. In July, General Scott ordered several of the smaller camps near Red Clay and Cleveland consolidated with other camps.[58]

Physicians were hired by emigration officials to attend the sick in the camps. Interpreters were hired to assist the physicians in communicating with Cherokee patients. Vaccinations, probably for smallpox, were given to the Indians. Emigration officials had good reason for this. A group of Chickasaw Indians who had been removed the previous year by steamboat was exposed to smallpox when the steamer stopped at a river town on the lower Arkansas River. After the party reached the western camps, a smallpox epidemic swept across the Indian territory south of the Canadian and Arkansas Rivers. Over five hundred Choctaws and Chickasaws died.[59]

Missionaries visited the camps to provide comfort and to hold church services. Dr. Elizur Butler, one of the missionaries arrested in 1831 by the Georgia Guard, offered his services as a physician to the camps and on one of the detachments that left in the fall of 1838. In October, the *Missionary Herald* reported that Dr. Butler "had been employed by the chiefs to serve as physician for one of the companies of emigrants[. He] writes from near McMinnville, Tennessee, on the 10th of October that the Cherokees were suffering severely from sickness. It was estimated by those having the best opportunity to judge, that two thousand or more, out of 16,000, had died since they were taken from their homes to the camps in June last; that is one eighth of the whole number, in less than four months."[60]

In late July, word leaked out to the public that there was much suffering in the camps. But Scott wrote Secretary of War Joel R. Poinsett on July 27, "The troops and Indians, in all their camps, continue to enjoy good general health." Scott's denial of widespread illness was published in the papers.[61] Reports from eyewitnesses visiting the camps—including the directing physician of Cherokee emigration, J. W. Lide—contradicted Scott. Dr. Lide's report is included in the chapter titled "For the Comfort and Well-being of This People."

Fall and Winter Emigration of 1838–39

At the approach of September 1, the deadline for the detachments to move under John Ross's management, the Cherokees made nervous preparations for the start. Scott had consolidated several of the camps around Cleveland and the Cherokee Agency in Charleston and was allowing limited movement among the camps. Families separated during the collection sought each other in the camps and tried to unite as best they could to travel in family groups. Leading Cherokees organized land detachments varying in size from 650 people—Treaty Party sympathizers led by John Adair Bell and Lieutenant Edward Deas—to 1,766 people—led by Peter and James Hilderbrand. The smallest of the fourteen detachments to leave in the fall of 1838 numbered about 230 people, under the direction of John Drew and John Golden Ross. It departed on December 5 by boat. This was the detachment that John and Quatie Ross joined. A small detachment of Cherokees also left from North Carolina, but very little is known about that party.[62]

Each of the land detachments under the management of John and Lewis Ross had a conductor, an assistant conductor, one or two physicians, one or two interpreters, one or two commissary agents, managers, and two or more wagon masters. Some also had chaplains. According to Ross's expense claims, there was one wagon for every twenty people, and ten horses per wagon. So, for a detachment of twelve hundred people, there were approximately sixty wagons and six hundred horses. Teams of oxen were also hired for the trips. Some of the Cherokees were able to bring their own horses. Some had managed to grab a few personal belongings as they were dragged from their homes by the soldiers. A few lucky Cherokees had been allowed to go back to retrieve personal items. Many of those belongings were loaded on to the wagons, making it necessary for some Cherokees to walk. Other belongings were carried on their owners' backs.[63]

Rebecca Neugin was only three years old when she and her family left for the West. She was interviewed by historian Grant Foreman when she was quite old. Her recollections of the Trail of Tears were from information given her by her mother:

> After they took us away my mother begged them to let her go back and get some bedding. So they let her go back and she brought what bedding and a few cooking utensils she could carry and had to leave behind all of our other household possessions. My father had a wagon pulled by two spans of oxen to haul us in. Eight of my brothers and sisters and two or three widow women and children rode with us. My brother Dick who was a good deal older than I was walked along with a long whip which he popped over the backs of the oxen and drove them all the way. My father and mother walked all the way also. The people got so tired of eating salt pork on the journey that my father would walk through the woods as we traveled, hunting for turkeys and deer which he brought into camp to feed us. Camp was usually made at some place where water was to be had and when we stopped and prepared to cook our food other emigrants who had been driven from their homes without opportunity to secure cooking utensils came to our camp to use our pots and kettles. There was much sickness among the emigrants and a great many little children died of whooping cough.[64]

In October 1897, a Franklin, Kentucky, newspaper published an article by one of Ross's assistants, Captain H. B. Henegar.

He recalled his experience on the trail, although he recorded a few facts incorrectly:

> The Indians all went the same route. We crossed the Tennessee at the mouth of the Hiwassee, at Blythe's Ferry, went across Walden's Ridge to Pikeville, thence to McMinnville, thence over to Nashville. After crossing the river there we went to Hopkinsville, Kentucky, crossing the Ohio River at Golconda, thence through Southern Illinois to Green's Ferry, on the Mississippi. Our detachment was stopped twenty miles from the river, at Gore's encampment, for those ahead to get across the Mississippi. After the way was opened we went to the river and commenced to cross and were detained over three weeks. I had charge of those left on the east side. After that we continued our journey through Southern Missouri, by way of Springfield, thence to the Nation, arriving at Park Hill, where John Ross had located himself, on March 25, 1839. The various detachments disbanded when we reached the Nation and went to different localities.[65]

The detachments under Ross's management did not all go the same route. Henegar served as wagon master for the Richard Taylor detachment, which crossed the Tennessee River at Vann's Town (near what is now Harrison, Tennessee) and made its way across the Cumberland Plateau through McMinnville, then joined what is called the northern route. The James Brown/Lewis Hilderbrand detachment had left earlier and followed approximately the same route. Most of the Ross-managed detachments that departed in the fall crossed the Tennessee River at Blythe's Ferry, crossed Walden's Ridge and the Cumberland Plateau, made their way to Nashville, then joined the northern route. From Tennessee, the northern route went north through Kentucky, southern Illinois, Missouri, and the northeastern corner of Arkansas and into Indian territory. The first detachment under Ross's management left in early October from Fort Payne, Alabama, and traveled by what is called the southern route. The southern route crossed the Tennessee River at Guntersville, Alabama, proceeded into Kentucky, crossed the Mississippi River at the Iron Banks, and then entered Indian territory. The final party under Ross was the relatively small Drew detachment, which carried Ross and his wife by water.[66]

Martin Davis drove a wagon pulled by a team of oxen for one of the detachments traveling overland on the northern route. On December 26, 1838, he wrote a letter home to his father, Daniel Davis of Dahlonega, Georgia, expressing concern for how slowly the emigration was going. He said he had spent three weeks in the Mississippi swamps just four miles from the river, and that he thought it might be another month before the party could cross the river because of the ice. He feared it might not reach Arkansas until March.

I take this opportunity to inform you I am well at present I ought to have wrote sooner but I have been in bad health ever since I passed Galconda [Golconda], Ill. with the cramp colic but I have got entirely well You have no doubt heard by this time about the accident which happened to our Detachment in crossing the Ohio River at Galconda The ferry boat is carried by steam across the river viz the way of Berry's Ferry Well to hand the boat had reached the bank of the river and the wagons and load taken off and on starting back to the east bank for another load they had gotten about thirty yards from the west bank when the boiler burst and scalded a great many persons There were only two killed at all one a white man the other a Cherokee. One was from our Detachment. This happened after I crossed the river in the evening.

On the morning following There is the coldest weather in Illinois I ever experienced anywhere The streams are all frozen over something like eight or twelve inches thick We are compelled to cut through the ice to get water for ourselves and animals It snows here every two or three days at the fartherest We are now camped in Mississippi swamp four miles from the river and there is no possible chance of crossing the river for the numerous quantity of ice that comes floating down the river every day.[67]

Newspapers carried accounts of the progress of the Cherokees. On January 26, 1839, the *New York Observer* published a sighting by someone from Maine who was traveling in the area and spotted the Cherokees:

2,000

We met several detachments in the southern part of Kentucky on the 4th, 5th and 6th of December. The last detachment which we passed on the 7th embraced rising two thousand Indians with horses and mules in proportion. The forward part of the train we found just pitching their tents for the night, and notwithstanding some thirty or forty waggons were already stationed, we found the road literally filled with the procession for about three miles in length. The sick and feeble were carried in waggons—about as comfortable for traveling as a New England ox cart with a covering over it—a great many ride on horseback and multitudes go on foot—even aged females, apparently nearly ready to drop into the grave, were traveling with heavy burdens attached to the back—on the sometimes frozen ground, and sometimes muddy streets, with no covering for the feet except what nature had given them. We were some hours making our way through the crowd, which brought us in close contact with the wagons and multitude, so much that we felt fortunate to find ourselves freed from the crowd without leaving any part of our carriage. We learned from the inhabitants on the road where the Indians passed, that they buried

buried 14-15 every day

fourteen or fifteen at every stopping place, and they make a journey of ten miles per day on an average.[68]

The official records don't support the figure of fourteen or fifteen deaths per attachment per day. At that rate, 90 percent of the Cherokees would have died before reaching Indian territory. The hardest hit were children and the elderly.

Two elderly Cherokees who lost their lives on the trail were Whitepath and Fly Smith. A respected leader, Whitepath fought at the battle of Horseshoe Bend and originally opposed the establishment of a Cherokee constitution and central government run by well-to-do mixed-bloods. But Whitepath later became a respected member of the Cherokee Council and served on the seven-member management committee for Cherokee Removal. Along with Elijah Hicks, he was one of the principal Cherokee leaders of the second detachment to leave Tennessee in the fall of 1838. By the time the Hicks/Whitepath detachment neared Hopkinsville, Kentucky, one of the ration stops along the northern route, Chief Whitepath and Fly Smith, another prominent local leader, were both gravely ill. They died shortly after reaching Hopkinsville. Whitepath, Fly Smith, and several other Cherokees were buried near the road. Their graves were marked by a white flag so those who followed could stop and pay their respects to their beloved elders.[69] Their graves are now protected in the Trail of Tears Commemorative Park in Hopkinsville.

Most of the detachments following the northern route crossed the Mississippi River on Green's ferry from Willard Landing in Illinois to Moccasin Springs in Missouri. The ferry crossing was located about ten miles north of Cape Girardeau. Due to ice on the river and snow on the roads, several detachments had to stop and camp on both sides of the river. Those camps were hit by epidemics. One of the many who died in the camps at Moccasin Springs was a young woman

epidemics

35

the whites called Princess Otahki. Through research, she was later identified as Nancy Bushyhead Walker Hilderbrand, the wife of Lewis Hilderbrand and sister of the Reverend Jesse Bushyhead. Her marked grave at the Trail of Tears State Park in Missouri serves as a destination for modern pilgrims on the trail. But while tragedy struck the Bushyhead family after it crossed the Missouri River, so did a joyful event. A daughter, Eliza Missouri Bushyhead, was born to the Reverend Jesse and Eliza Bushyhead on January 3, 1839. Against the odds, the infant Eliza survived the Trail of Tears and became an important leader of the Cherokee Nation in Tahlequah before she died at the age of eighty-one.[70]

Ross's Last Water Detachment

The last detachment, conducted by John Drew, left by water from the Cherokee Agency at Charleston on December 5, 1838, and arrived in the Cherokee Nation West on March 18, 1839. Among the 231 people in the party were John Ross and his wife, Quatie. They took the canal around Muscle Shoals, Alabama. Ross purchased a steamboat, the *Victoria*, for ten thousand dollars in Tuscumbia. The *Victoria* had been used earlier in the Cherokee emigration. At Paducah, Kentucky, Ross was called away when word arrived that some of the other detachments had stopped because of rumors that the roads through Missouri were impassable and supplies unavailable. Ross also had to resolve a dispute between conductor Chuwaloskee, also called Chooalooka, and his assistant, J. D. Wafford. Ross appointed a Mr. Clark to take charge of the detachment.[71]

After resolving the two crises, Ross returned to the boat at Paducah, and the detachment set off again. He later wrote that "within a week from that time my children became motherless and the remains of Mrs. Ross left in a strange land." Quatie Ross, John's wife of many years, was buried along the trail. The party continued by water to Arkansas and past Fort Smith to the mouth of the Illinois River. From there, it traveled the last forty miles by wagon.[72]

In a letter dated November 9, 1838, from Athens, Tennessee, Winfield Scott stated that he was informed by Indian authorities that 12,608 Cherokees had emigrated under Ross's management but that only 11,721 were officially counted. The discrepancy of 887 souls was caused by the many individuals and families who joined the detachments after the muster rolls were closed.[73]

Arrival in the West

In 1831, in preparation of the Choctaw emigration, Colonel Matthew Arbuckle of the Seventh Infantry sent Lieutenant James R. Stephenson to the old Fort Towson in anticipation of re-garrisoning the post on the Red River in the western territory. Towson would be used as a supply depot and a destination point for emigrating Choctaws. Arbuckle also sent Lieutenant Gabriel Rains and a five-man detachment to reopen old Fort Gibson as a supply post for the emigrating Indians. When the Choctaws began to arrive in 1831, Lieutenant Stephenson became supply agent for the emigrants. He was transferred to Fort Gibson and was later promoted to captain. He continued his role as receiving agent for the western territory through the Cherokee emigrations of 1836-39. It was his job to officially receive arriving detachments from the officers in charge and to muster them for counting at the end of their journey. Stephenson was also responsible for furnishing new arrivals with subsistence for a year—in accordance with the terms of the Treaty of New Echota—to help them become adjusted to their new lives.[74]

The Cherokees who arrived in the Cherokee Nation West during the winter of 1838-39 faced many challenges. The "old settlers," many of whom had emigrated fifteen or twenty years earlier, had established their own government and expected the new emigrants to obey their laws. However, just prior to removal, John Ross's party passed a resolution carrying its government intact to the West. The Treaty Party also expected to play a role in any new government that might be formed. Initial efforts to reconcile the three parties failed. Violence erupted on June 22, 1839, when Major Ridge, John Ridge, and Elias Boudinot were murdered near their homes in the Arkansas Territory. John Adair Bell and Boudinot's brother Stand Watie narrowly escaped the same fate after they were warned of the other murders. The murders were in retaliation for the roles the Treaty Party members had played in the 1835 Treaty of New Echota and the removal and for suspected intrigues with the old settlers. Although John Ross was initially suspected as being involved in the murders, the participants later cleared him.[75]

There were reports of many illnesses and deaths after the Cherokees reached their new lands in the West. Among the eastern and western Cherokees James Mooney interviewed in the late nineteenth century was J. D. Wafford, one of the detachment leaders. Mooney reported that "hundreds of others died soon after their arrival in Indian Territory, from sickness and exposure on the journey." In February 1839, smallpox broke out among the Osage Indians, who were preparing to vacate lands recently set aside for the arrival of the Cherokees. The outbreak continued well into March. Arbuckle, by then the general in command of the entire Southwest, ordered all Osages except those with smallpox to leave within six days.[76] The vaccinations in the Cherokee camps earlier in the summer may have prevented a few deaths.

An elderly woman who experienced the Trail of Tears as a youth later told historian Grant Foreman that life was very difficult for many Cherokees after their arrival in the West. Most had left their belongings in the East and were now destitute.

Many had to start over from scratch by using skills from earlier days. She recalled,

> Very few of the Indians had been able to bring any of their household effects or kitchen utensils with them and the old people who knew how, made what they called dirt pots and dirt bowls. To make them they took clay and formed it in the shape desired and turned these bowls over the fire and smoked them and when they were done they would hold water and were very useful. We could cook in them and use them to hold food. In the same way they made dishes to eat out of and then they made wooden spoons and for a number of years after we arrived we had to use these crude utensils. After awhile as we were able, we gradually picked up glazed china ware until we had enough to take the place of the substitutes. We had no shoes and those that wore anything wore moccasins made out of deer hide and the men wore leggins made of deer hide.[77]

Meanwhile, the Cherokee leaders quickly set about rebuilding their nation. Ethan Allan Hitchcock, a visitor to the western nation in 1841, witnessed children going to schools, trees being girdled to open up pasture and farmland, cattle-ranching operations, and other industry. He visited the capital of Tahlequah with its supreme and circuit courts, public houses where food was provided free by the government, and houses for the principal chief and the Cherokee Council and Committee. The Cherokees also reestablished their press, established institutions of higher learning, and elected John Ross principal chief. He remained in that position until his death in 1866.[78] In the East, an estimated one thousand Cherokees had escaped into the hills and mountains to avoid removal. Some of those who emigrated, like the war hero Junaluska, became disgruntled with life in the West and made their way home. Some

8,000

Cherokees received certificates allowing them to remain in the Southeast, and some who had remained in the East later enrolled for emigration to the West. For many years, William Holland Thomas and the eastern Cherokees faced multiple political and legal battles to secure their permanent residency and to clarify their legal status.[79]

Aftermath

In March 1839, Dr. Elizur Butler, who had accompanied the Cherokees west on the Elijah Hicks detachment, wrote a letter to the *Hamilton Gazette* concerning the number of deaths that occurred in the camps and in the emigrating detachments. He estimated the number of deaths to be between four thousand and forty-six hundred. Over the years, many historians and writers have used his estimates and those of James Mooney. Russell Thornton, who has studied the mortality rates of the Cherokees during and immediately after the 1838 removal, believes the number was closer to eight thousand. Thornton's estimate takes into account those who died on the trail, in the camps, and after arriving in the West.[80]

Because records of deaths were not kept in the camps or after arrival in the West, it will never be known for sure how many perished. The emigration was such an ordeal, and so many innocent lives were lost, that the Cherokees subsequently named the journey *Nu-No-Du-Na-Tlo-Hi-Lu*, literally, "the Trail Where They Cried." To later generations, it has become known as the Trail of Tears.[81]

It has been estimated that as many as a hundred thousand Native Americans were relocated west of the Mississippi River from their eastern homelands during the first half of the nineteenth century. A large percentage of these were members of the five civilized tribes—the Chickasaws, the Choctaws, the Cherokees, the Creeks, and the Seminoles—along with remnants of other southeastern Indian groups. Most resettlements occurred in the decade following the passage of the 1830 Indian Removal Act, although some occurred prior to its passage and some later. The emigration of the other southeastern tribes is not as well known to the public as the Cherokee Removal but was just as tragic. The Choctaws are said to have lost 15 percent of their population as a result of their removal. The Creeks and Seminoles are believed to have suffered a mortality rate of about 50 percent. Many of these deaths occurred in the period immediately following removal. For example, of the ten thousand or more Creeks who emigrated in 1836-37, thirty-five hundred died of "bilious fevers."[82]

The removal of the southeastern Native Americans west of the Mississippi is one of the great tragedies in United States history. While each of the five civilized tribes has shown incredible resilience in fighting back from the decimating effects of their removal, the terrible injustice of broken treaties, discriminatory laws, unenforced court rulings, land grabbing, and ethnocentric intolerance, all done in the name of western expansion, will forever be a blight on the memory of the American people.

I Hope My Bones Will Not Be Deserted by You

1821 and 1829

During the 1820s, pressure from the federal government and the citizens of Georgia made it increasingly difficult for Cherokees to remain in that state. Many began to consider the advantages of selling their homes and moving west, where they could more readily retain their traditional beliefs. As an increasing number of Cherokees started to sell, usually under duress, the Cherokee National Committee and Council resolved to strengthen the Cherokees' resistance to offers to buy their property by placing harsh punishments on those caught selling. According to Cherokee tradition, land could not be owned by an individual but belonged to the whole tribe. One victim of the Cherokees' harsh punishment was Alexander McCoy, who sought an emigration officer to assess the value of his holdings. For his disloyalty to the Cherokee cause, he was stripped of his post as clerk of the National Council. John Ridge was chosen to replace him.[1]

In 1821, the Cherokees enacted a law placing a fine of $150 and forfeiture of land improvements for selling to outsiders. Then, in October 1829, a law was passed that resurrected an even older penalty for selling land inside the national boundaries. The new law made death the penalty for such an action.

The first excerpt below is the text of the 1821 law, as reprinted in the *Cherokee Phoenix and Indians' Advocate* on April 3, 1828. It showed John Ross's signature as president of the National Council, Alexander McCoy's signature as clerk for the council, and the signatures of Path Killer and Charles Hicks. The second excerpt is an article from the same newspaper announcing the 1829 law and quoting a respected elder, Womankiller, who spoke at the council in support of the law. The article ran on October 28, 1829.

Excerpts from the
Cherokee Phoenix and Indians' Advocate
on laws preventing the sale of Cherokee lands

EXCERPT 1

New Town, Oct. 27, 1821

Resolved by the National Committee and Council, That any person or persons, whatsoever, who shall choose to emigrate to the Arkansas country, and shall sell the improvements he or they may be in possession of, to any person or persons whatsoever, he or they, so disposing of their improvements, shall forfeit and pay unto the Cherokee nation the sum of one hundred and fifty dollars; and be it further resolved, that any person or persons, whatsoever, who shall purchase any improvement from person or persons so emigrating; he or they so offending, shall also forfeit and pay a fine of one hundred and fifty dollars to the nation, to be collected by the marshal of the district.[2]

Saturday Oct. 24th

On motion of Choonnagkee of Chickamauga District, an old law, making death the penalty for selling any lands in treaty, without the authority of the nation, was committed to writing. The bill was adopted.

Womankiller, of Hickory Log District, who is probably more than eighty years of age, rose and spoke substantially as follows in reference to the bill:

My Children,

Permit me to call you so as I am an old man, and has lived a long time, watching the well being of this Nation. I love your lives, and wish our people to increase on the land of our fathers. The bill before you is to punish wicked men, who may arise to cede away our country contrary to the consent of the Council. It is a good law—it will not kill the innocent but the guilty. I feel the importance of the subject, and am glad the law has been suggested. My companions, men of renown, in Council, who now sleep in the dust, spoke the same language, and I now stand on the verge of the grave to bear witness to their love of country. My sun of existence is fast approaching to its sitting, and my aged bones will soon be laid under ground, and I wish them laid in the bosom of this earth we have received from our fathers who had it from the Great Being above. When I shall sleep in forgetfulness, I hope my bones will not be deserted by you. I do not speak this in fear of any of you, as the evidence of your attachment to the country is proved by the bill now before your consideration, I am indeed told, that the Government of the U States will spoil their treaties with us and sink our National Council under their feet. —It may be so, but it shall not be with our consent, or by the misconduct of our people. We hold them by the golden chain of friendship, made when our friendship was worth a price, and if they act the tyrant and kill us for our lands, we shall, in a state of unoffending innocence, sleep with the thousands of our departed people. My feeble limits will not allow me to stand longer. I can say no more, but before I sit, allow me to tell you that I am in favor of the bill.[3]

FIRST BLOOD SHED
BY THE GEORGIANS
February 1830

As THE POPULATION of Georgia grew during the early nineteenth century, the Cherokees reported a number of intruders on their land. These were white men who moved to the Cherokee Nation illegally. Some were squatters, while others purchased land from emigrating Cherokees in violation of Cherokee law. The discovery of gold in the Cherokee mountains in 1829 also brought an influx of trespassers, many of disreputable character. Bands of thieves and cattle rustlers roamed the Cherokee countryside on horseback. In one reported incident, they went to the home of an elderly woman and asked for some beans and corn. When she explained that she had nothing to sell, they set her woods on fire. These bands of thieves were called "poney clubs" by the Cherokees.[1]

The Cherokees complained to Colonel Hugh Montgomery, the Cherokee agent; to Captain Brooks, commander of the

Georgia Guard; and to other authorities. But little was done. The Cherokees came to suspect that the intruders were supported in their actions by some of the local authorities.[2]

Located in Georgia near the Alabama border was a pocket of territory the Cherokees had obtained from the Creeks in 1821. The federal government recognized Cherokee ownership of this land in 1826. But Georgia, not accepting Cherokee ownership, took possession of the land. When the Cherokees appealed to the federal government, General John Coffee, a friend of President Jackson, was sent to investigate. Coffee held hearings on the contested land and decided that Georgia had no claim to it. Coffee told the Cherokees it was the duty of the principal chief to throw the Georgians off the land. John Ross reportedly delegated the task to Major Ridge.

After painting his body red and placing a buffalo head atop his own head, Major Ridge rode to the disputed territory with a group of Cherokees. They visited seventeen or eighteen white families, giving each time to leave its stolen house. Then the Cherokees set fire to the structures and ordered the whites to leave Cherokee land permanently.[3]

Major Ridge and most of the men returned home. However, four members of the party stayed behind at one of the houses, where they had discovered some whiskey. The next morning, a party of twenty-five whites found them drunk. They were bound, beaten, and placed on horses, to be taken to Georgia. One man, Chewoyee, kept falling off his horse. He eventually died, perhaps due to a fall. Two of the Cherokees escaped, one of whom was stabbed as he fled. The fourth Cherokee was taken to the Carroll County Jail. The whites made threats to burn down the homes of John Ross and Major Ridge, but armed Cherokees quickly surrounded those houses.[4]

News of the raid spread quickly. Governor Gilmer and Georgia newspapers protested the raids by the Cherokees and claimed that the white families ejected from the Cherokee homes had been savagely evicted. They relished the opportunity to describe Major Ridge's costume.[5]

Elias Boudinot wrote several editorials in the *Cherokee Phoenix and Indians' Advocate* about the problems the Cherokees were having with intruders. Included below is one from the February 10, 1830, issue of the paper. Boudinot reports on the aftermath of Major Ridge's raid on the families of squatters and appeals for calm.[6]

Editorial by Elias Boudinot
from the *Cherokee Phoenix and Indians' Advocate*

FIRST BLOOD SHED BY THE GEORGIANS!!

. . . We have been told by a gentleman who passed this place as an express to the agent, from the principal chief, that a Cherokee has, at last, been *killed* by the intruders, and three more taken bound into Georgia! We are not prepared this week to give the public any particulars respecting this unpleasant affair. The general facts are, however, these, the particulars of which will be given in our next. A company of Cherokees, among whom were some of our most respectable citizens, constrained by the repeated aggressions and insults of a number of intruders, who had settled themselves far in the country, & likewise by the frequent losses sustained by many of our citizens in cattle and horses from their own countrymen, who are leagued in wickedness with our civilized brothers, started the other day, under the authority of the Principal Chief to correct, at least part of the evil. They were out two days in which time they arrested four Cherokee horse-thieves. These received exemplary punishment. They found also 17 families of intruders, living, we *believe*, in Cherokee houses. These they ordered out and after safely taking out their beddings, chairs &c. the houses were set on fire. In no instance was the least violence used on the part of the Cherokees. When the company returned home, five of them tarried on the way, who, we are sorry to say, had become intoxicated. In this situation, they were found by a company of intruders, twenty five in number—One was killed, & three taken into Georgia.

Thus a circumstance, which we have for a long time dreaded, and which has been brought about by the neglect of the executive to remove the great nuisance to the Cherokees, has happened. We are nevertheless, glad, that the injury received is on the side of this nation. It has been the desire of our enemies that the Cherokees may be urged to some desperate act—thus far this desire has never been realized, and we hope, notwithstanding the great injury now sustained, their wonted forbearance will be continued. If our word will have any weight with our countrymen in this very trying time, we would say, *forbear, forbear*—revenge not, but leave vengeance to him "to whom vengeance belongeth."

P.S. On last Saturday, it was reported, that a large company of Georgians were on their way to arrest Mr. Ross and Major Ridge. We think it not improbable that an attempt of that kind will be made. If so, self defence, on the part of the Cherokees, many of whom we understand, were at Ross's and Ridge's, would undoubtedly be justifiable.[7]

THE ENEMIES
OF GEORGIA
1831

THE REVEREND SAMUEL WORCESTER was sent by the American Board of Commissioners for Foreign Missions to the Brainerd Mission in 1825. Soon afterward, he was sent to the new mission at New Echota, where he helped arrange for the purchase of the *Cherokee Phoenix* printing press and assumed the role of coeditor of the *Phoenix* with Elias Boudinot.[1]

Worcester became a strong advocate of Cherokee rights on the subjects of removal and of laws passed by the state of Georgia seeking to destroy the sovereignty of the Cherokee Nation. Colonel Thomas McKenney, head of the Bureau of Indian Affairs, wrote a letter of complaint to the American Board of Commissioners for Foreign Missions accusing Worcester of interfering with the press and of writing inflammatory articles about government officials and other public men. The board stood by Worcester and supported him against the claims of McKenney.[2]

In September 1830, Methodist missionaries in the Cherokee country called a meeting at the Chattooga campground, where they drew up a resolution that supported the Cherokees and noted the injustices practiced by Georgia and the Jackson administration. Eight Methodist missionaries including James J. Trott and Dickson C. McLeod signed the resolution. In December, Moravian, Congregationalist, Baptist, and Presbyterian missionaries met at New Echota and drew up a similar resolution supporting the Cherokees. Among the signers of the interdenominational resolution were Samuel Worcester, Elizur Butler, Daniel Butrick, John Thompson, and Isaac Proctor for the American Board. Dickson C. McLeod was also in attendance at the December meeting.[3]

As the missionaries were meeting to draw up their resolution, the Georgia legislature was passing a law prohibiting white men from remaining in Cherokee lands within the state. On March 1, 1831, the law took effect. It required all white male adults residing within the Cherokee Nation to take an oath of allegiance to the state. They also had to obtain a license or permit from the governor to reside in the Cherokee Nation. The law was aimed particularly at the missionaries stationed at the New Echota, Carmel, Haweis, and Hightower Missions. At a meeting soon after the law was passed, the missionaries at those four missions decided not to be intimidated. They declared that "taking an oath of allegiance is out of the question."[4]

In March 1831, Georgia began a series of arrests of troublemakers in the Cherokee Nation. On March 12, missionaries Samuel Worcester, John Thompson, and Isaac Proctor were arrested by the Georgia Guard. They were soon released by Judge Augustin Clayton on the grounds that the laws did not apply to the missionaries, as they were agents of the government because of their involvement in administering the Indian Civilization Fund. Clayton also felt

Worcester was exempt from the law because he was a postmaster. Governor George R. Gilmer promptly wrote to the postmaster general, William T. Barry, and had Worcester dismissed from his postmaster duties. John Eaton, the secretary of war, assured Governor Gilmer that the government did not consider the missionaries to be its agents.[5]

Some of the missionaries began to reconsider their situation. Butrick, Proctor, and Thompson moved out of state. The missionaries subsequently thought they were immune from arrest, since they no longer officially resided in the state and carried out their business at the missions only through frequent visits.[6]

In May, Governor Gilmer wrote Worcester warning him that he would arrest anyone who did not take the oath of allegiance to the state. Gilmer ordered Colonel John W. A. Sanford to deliver the letter and to arrest Worcester if he didn't leave Georgia immediately. However, Sanford took pity on the plight of Worcester and his family. Ann Worcester and the couple's new baby, Jerusha, were too ill to travel. Sanford could not bring himself to arrest Worcester under the circumstances.[7]

In early July, Worcester, Elizur Butler, and James J. Trott were arrested. When Dickson McLeod, who did not reside in Georgia, as the others did, came to protest the arrests, he, too, was arrested. Martin Wells, another missionary who protested the arrests, was beaten on the head with a stick.[8]

Eventually, Worcester was released on a writ of habeas corpus. His bond agreement required that he leave the state until his hearing in September. Worcester went to Brainerd, in Tennessee, leaving his sick family in New Echota because the danger of rearrest was so great. Meanwhile, Jerusha died. Worcester did not receive word of her death until after the funeral. Two days following his return home, the Georgia Guard came to arrest him a second time. He was later released when Colonel Nelson of the Georgia Guard learned of the circumstances that had brought him home.[9]

Worcester's trial was held on September 16. Eleven men, including Worcester and Butler, were quickly found guilty of violating Georgia law. They were sentenced to four years of hard labor.[10]

On Sunday morning, September 18, they set out on their march to the Milledgeville prison. When they reached Milledgeville, Governor Gilmer offered the eleven prisoners pardons if they would take the oath to abide by Georgia laws, abandon their missionary labors, and withdraw from the state. Only Worcester and Butler refused the terms. Worcester was shackled and marched to jail.[11]

During his months in prison, he took the opportunity to study carpentry and cabinet making and borrowed books to study medicine. Later, when Ann Worcester had recovered from her illness, Elias Boudinot raised money from several prominent Cherokees, including John Ross, to finance her trip to Milledgeville to visit her husband in prison. She was accompanied by Mrs. Butler.[12]

The plight of the missionaries aroused wide sympathy. Supporters of the Cherokee cause encouraged the missionaries to take their case before the United States Supreme Court. The case was argued by William Wirt and John Sargeant before the court in February 1832. No one appeared before the court on behalf of Georgia. On March 3, Chief Justice John Marshall pronounced the decision of the court in favor of the missionaries. The decision declared null and void the laws of Georgia that sought to extend the state's jurisdiction over the Cherokee country. However, the Georgia courts refused to obey the Supreme Court or to order the release of Butrick and Worcester. Appeals to Governor Wilson Lumpkin went unheeded.[13]

In November, the missionaries decided to ask the Supreme Court for further process in hopes of gaining their release. But the governor convinced the Prudential Committee of the

American Board to withdraw the case. The American Board subsequently wrote to the missionaries that it would not proceed with further litigation. When Worcester realized the futility of the case, he withdrew the charges, and Governor Lumpkin issued a proclamation setting the missionaries free.[14]

Worcester and his family moved back to Brainerd for several months. They left for the Cherokee territory in the West on April 8, 1835, and arrived at Dwight Mission in late May. Worcester began new duties as a missionary and launched efforts to secure a new printing press.[15]

Dr. Butler served at Haweis until the mission premises were seized under Georgia law, after which he moved to the Brainerd Mission. He remained there until September 1836, when he moved to Red Clay, about twenty miles east of Brainerd. At that time, about forty families lived at Red Clay, including several prominent Cherokees. National Councils had been held there for some time. Butler later emigrated west with the Cherokees, serving as a physician for one of the detachments.[16]

The Reverend Worcester wrote accounts of both of his arrests, as did some of the others. Below is his account of his second arrest, written on July 18, 1831. In it, he mentions some of the other missionaries involved, including James J. Trott, Dickson C. McLeod, Martin Wells, and Elizur Butler. Apparently, the Proctor in the account was not Isaac Proctor of the American Board.

Excerpt from the Reverend Samuel Worcester's account of his second arrest by the Georgia Guard

Early on Friday morning July 8, I with my guard joined Sergeant Brooks at . . . the house of a near neighbor and rode thense ten miles to where Col. Nelson was[. The detachment commanded by Brooks that arrested Worcester was part of a larger detachment commanded by Colonel Nelson.] There I found the Rev. Mr. Trott, a Methodist missionary who has a Cherokee family and a Cherokee by the name of Proctor. Proctor was chained to the wall of the house by the neck & had another chain around his ancle. He had been arrested on Tuesday on the charge of digging for gold, chained the first night by the ancle only, the second & third by the neck to the wall & by the ancle to Mr. Trott. Mr. Trott was arrested on Wednesday & taken on horseback about ten miles to where Col. Nelson then was. He had been before arrested & was under bonds to answer at Court for the offence of residing in the nation without licence & now was taken again, & having committed the second offence by returning to his family while the cause was pending. On Thursday, he & Proctor were marched on foot 22 miles to the place where I found them, Proctor being chained by the neck to the waggon. This manner of treatment, I suppose, was occasioned by his having resistance when arrested and afterwards attempted to escape.

When I was arrested, Sergeant Brooks enquired the state of my family & when told that Mrs. Worcester was still confined to her bed, remarked that he regretted that Col. Nelson was not himself present, implying, as I understood him, that if he were he probably would not arrest me under such circumstances. When we arrived where Col. Nelson was I requested Mr. Brooks to mention to him the state in which he found us which he very readily promised to do but certainly had not fulfilled his promise when I heard him say that I was to go on to the Head Quarters, i.e. to this place. Perceiving therefore that the state of my family was not to be regarded, I said no more.

We were then marched on foot 22 miles to the same place from which Mr. Trott & Mr. Proctor were taken the day before, Proctor being again chained to the waggon. We had proceeded about three miles when we met Messrs. McLeod & Wells, Methodist clergymen not residing within the charter of Georgia. With leave of Col. Nelson, they turned & rode along some distance in our company. In conversation, Mr. McLeod asked Mr. Trott whether he had been chained the preceeding night, & being answered in the affirmative, asked if it were according to law to chain a prisoner who manifested no disposition to escape. Mr. Trott said he thought not, but that we ought not to blame those under who[se] charge we were as they were obliged to act according to orders. Mr. McLeod remarked, "It seems they proceed more by orders than by laws." This gave offence. A few words had passed between Mr. McLeod & some of the guard when Col. Nelson rode up & being told of the remark asked Mr. McLeod where he resides. He replied "in Tennessee." Col. Nelson with a curse ordered him to "____ of[f]." Mr. McLeod turning his horse said ["]I will, sir, if it is your command" but added hastily as he afterwards said, "You will hear from me again." He was then riding away when the Col. ordered him to halt & then to dismount & lead his horse along in the rear. He then enquired of Mr. Trott whether this was one of their circuit riders. Mr. Trott answered "yes." Mr. McLeod's horse was then taken from him & delivered to Mr. Wells and he was declared a prisoner & ordered to walk on with the rest. For a short distance, Brooks compelled him to keep the center of the road through mire & water threatening to thrust him through with the bayonette if he turned aside. In the mean time he was heaping upon all our heads a load of tremendous curses & reviling missionaries and all ministers of the Gospel in language which for profanity and obscenity could not be exceeded. The words of our Savior he turned into ridi-cule—Fear not—said he tauntingly, Fear not, "little flock, for it is your Father's good pleasure to give you the kingdom." The manner in which these words were uttered did not prevent me at least from rejoicing in the consolation they afford. Brooks was the chief speaker & exceeded all though some others joined him in his revilings.

Another circumstance afterwards occurred, which was related

to me by Mr. Thompson, who was eye witness. Mr. Wells, after Mr. McLeod's arrest, pursued his journey in the opposite direction till he met Mr. Thompson riding in the same direction with the guard. He then turned and rode in company with Mr. T. intending to see what should become of Mr. McLeod and to render him any assistance in his power. After some time they came up with the guard. When Col. Nelson saw Mr. Wells, he ordered him to ride out of his sight either before or behind, threatening violence if he did not. Mr. Wells, without replying, fell back a little & followed on. Col. Nelson cut a stick and walking up to Mr. Wells gave him a severe blow on the head. Mr. Wells then said he had a right to travel the public road & should do it. He persevered accordingly & rode on till he came to a house where Mr. McLeod requested him to stop. I know not what offence Mr. Wells had given unless that in conversation with me, he had expressed strong disapprobation of the policy of the State of Georgia & the course pursued by the Executive of the United States.

Towards the end of our days journey, Mr. McLeod was afflicted with a severe pain in the hips & knees to which he had been subject & requested the privilege of riding. Col. Nelson sent his answer, that Proctor at first thought that he could not walk, but afterwards got along very well.

At night the four prisoners were chained together by their ancle in pairs.

Sometime after we lay down, a small detachment arrived with Doctor [Elizur] Butler. He had been arrested at Haweis [Mission] on the preceeding day. After crossing a river, three or four miles from home, a chain was fastened by a padlock around his neck and at the other end to the neck of a horse buy the side of which he walked. Night soon came on. The horse was kept walking at a quick pace and Doctor Butler unable to see any obstruction which a rough road might present, and liable at any moment to fall and so to be dragged by the neck till the horse should stop. After walking some distance in the dark, on representing the danger of his situation, he was taken up behind the saddle, his chain being still fastened to the horse's neck & short enough to keep his neck close to the shoulder of the guard. In this situation the horse fell, both his riders fell under him and neither the horse nor either of the men could rise till others could come and, after ascertaining their situation by the sense of feeling, roll the horse over. Dr. Butler was considerably hurt, but the soldier more, having two ribs broken. After this, till they came to their lodgings, Dr. Butler was permitted to ride, while a soldier walked. In the mean time they lost their way in the woods. However, they found a fine knob of which they made a torch by striking fire, and by this means recovered their way. Their lodging place was only 14 miles from Dr. Butler's, but it was midnight when they arrived, well [drenched] with rain. When they lay down, the prisoner was chained to his bedstead by the ancle, the officer, however, putting a handkerchief around under the chain. The next day they had 35 miles or more to travel. Dr. Butler wore the chain on his neck but no longer fastened to a horse. He was occasionally permitted to ride, one or another of the soldiers walking in his stead. At night he was chained to Mr. McLeod and me.

On Friday morning we had to cross the Hightower river in a boat. As the prisoners with a part of the guard were crossing, Mr. Thompson was observed on the opposite side waiting to speak with us. At the same time Col. Nelson & Sergeant Brooks were observed in conversation. Brooks then called to those who were with us, charging them that no person should be allowed to speak with a prisoner privately, and no letter to be delivered unexamined.

Proctor was now mounted on his own horse which had been taken as a prize when he was arrested, wearing a chain as Dr. Butler had worn it the day before. He had a bag of clothes for a saddle and a rope halter instead of a bridle. No other one was chained. When we had travelled a considerable distance four of the soldiers were so kind as to walk four or five miles & allow the prisoners to ride, for which we were told they were afterwards abused by Brooks, who now had the command of the detachment, Col. Nelson having parted from them. Afterwards, Mr. Trott being likely to fail, was mounted on Proctor's horse in his stead. Still later Mr. McLeod, having become so lame that he could scarcely walk, solicited the privilege of riding. Brooks with much cursing compelled him to walk on. Afterwards, however, he ordered Mr. Trott to dismount, and placed Mr. McLeod in his stead. Our day's journey was 35 miles.

At night only Proctor was chained. Brooks having retired without giving any orders on the subject, and the officer who had the charge of us not being disposed to chain us.

The Sabbath came. We had 22 miles to travel. Remonstrance would on[ly] have irritated. We were under the command of armed men & must travel on. Mr. McLeod being utterly unable to walk was mounted on Proctor's horse. Mr. Trott was allowed to ride part of the way in the waggon and Dr. Butler & myself two or three miles on horse back.

Arrived here we were as a matter of course marched into camp under sound of fife and drum. We were then introduced to the jail, Brooks saying as we entered, "Here is w[h]ere all the enemies of Georgia have to land—Here and in Hell." Happily man has not the keyes of the everlasting prison. At night a white man who has a Cherokee family was added to our number.

On Monday Mr. Thompson & Mr. Wells came & requested an interview with us. Mr. Thomas [Thompson] was admitted under the restriction that no one should have any private conversation with us or receive any papers from us without their being inspected by Col. Nelson who has the present command. Col. Sanford being absent. Mr. Wells was refused admittance.

Mr. McLeod sent a note to Col. Nelson on Monday, requesting a personal interview. On Tuesday morning Col. Nelson sent for him & dismissed him. He was not permitted to return & bid us farewell.

On Saturday evening July 16 perceiving that we should probably spend the Sabbath here, we sent to Col. Nelson the following request.

"Col. Ch. H. Nelson

"Sir,

"If it be consistent with necessary regulations it would be a high gratification to some of your prisoners if Mr. Trott & Mr. Worcester might be permitted to hold a meeting tomorrow evening at some place where such of the guard & of the neighbors as are disposed might attend. If the favor can be granted, be so kind as to give us an answer as soon as convenient. We wish to be understood that we should all greatly desire the privilege of attending.

"(Signed), S. A. Worcester, J. J. Trott, Elizur Butler, Samuel Mayes."

This note was presently returned with the following written on the outside.

"We view the within request as an impertinent one. If your conduct be evidence of your character & the doctrines you wish to promulgate, we are sufficiently enlightened as to both. Our object is to restrain, not to facilitate their promulgation. If your object be true piety you can enjoy it where you are, were we hearers we would not be benefited, devoid as we are of confidence in your honesty.

"Signed C. H. Nelson."

From most of the individuals of the guard we have received no ill treatment, from some of them kindness. As was, however, perhaps to be expected in our circumstances, we have received some insults which it is trying for the spirit to bear. But we regard it as a testimony in our favor that when the desire is to torture us it is taken for granted that this can be best effected by uttering profane & obscene expressions in our ears.[17]

THAT PAPER CALLED
A TREATY
March 1836

MAJOR WILLIAM M. DAVIS was appointed by Secretary of War Lewis Cass to serve as an enrolling agent. His assignments included seeking out Cherokees who were willing to enroll for emigration to the West and assisting in the appraisal of the homes and property they must leave behind.

Davis was living in Cherokee country at the time the Treaty of New Echota was signed in December 1835. On March 5, 1836, he wrote Secretary Cass about his concerns over the actions of the Reverend John F. Schermerhorn, appointed by the Jackson administration to negotiate with the Cherokees, and about the manner in which the treaty was obtained.[1]

Report of Major William M. Davis
to Secretary of War Lewis Cass

I conceive that my duty to the President, to yourself, and to my country, reluctantly compels me to make a statement of facts in relation to a meeting of a small number of Cherokees at New Echota last December, who were met by Mr. Schermerhorn and articles of a general treaty entered into between them for the whole Cherokee Nation.

. . . I should not interpose in the matter at all but I discover that you do not receive impartial information on the subject; that you have to depend upon the *ex parte*, partial, and interested reports of a person who will not give you the truth. I will not be silent when I see that you are about to be imposed on by a gross and base betrayal of the high trust reposed in Rev. J. F. Schermerhorn by you. His conduct and course of policy was a series of blunders from first to last. . . . It has been wholly of a partisan character.

Sir, that paper . . . called a treaty is no treaty at all, because not sanctioned by the great body of the Cherokees and made without their participation or assent. I solemnly declare to you that upon its reference to the Cherokee people it would be instantly rejected by nine-tenths of them and I believe by nineteen-twentieths of them. There were not present at the conclusion of the treaty more than one hundred Cherokee voters, and not more than three hundred, including women and children, although the weather was everything that could be desired. The Indians had long been notified of the meeting, and blankets were promised to all who would come and vote for the treaty. The most cunning and artful means were resorted to to conceal the paucity of numbers present at the treaty. No enumeration of them was made by Schermerhorn. The business of making the treaty was transacted with a committee appointed by the Indians present, so as not to expose their numbers. The power of attorney under which the committee acted was signed only by the president and secretary of the meeting, so as not to disclose their weakness. . . . Mr. Schermerhorn's apparent design was to conceal the real number present and to impose on the public and the Government upon this point. The delegation taken to Washington by Mr. Schermerhorn had no more authority to make a treaty than any other dozen Cherokees accidentally picked up for that purpose. I now warn you and the President that if this paper of Schermerhorn's called a treaty is sent to the Senate and ratified you will bring trouble upon the Government and eventually destroy this (the Cherokee) nation. The Cherokees are a peaceable, harmless people, but you may drive them to desperation, and this treaty cannot be carried into effect except by the strong arm of force.[2]

YOUR FATE
IS DECIDED

March 1837

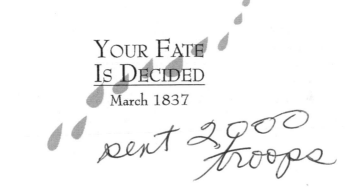

sent 2,000 troops

FEARING THERE MIGHT BE an armed resistance by the Cherokees, as there had been among the Creeks and Seminoles, the War Department sent General John E. Wool and two thousand United States troops to Cherokee country in early 1836. Wool's orders were to disarm the Cherokees and to enroll as many as possible for voluntary emigration. He was also charged with rounding up for emigration several hundred fugitive Creeks hiding in Cherokee territory.[1]

Wool went to the Valley River region of North Carolina and sought the assistance of Evan Jones, a respected Baptist missionary living among the Cherokees. Wool ordered Jones to help him disarm the Indians. Jones refused and was arrested by Wool, as were a few other men and women. Wool soon released them, but Jones was ordered to leave North Carolina.[2]

In September 1836, John Ross called for a General Council

of the Cherokees to discuss and protest the Treaty of New Echota. Wool allowed the council to be held, though he wrote the War Department that "no good will come of it, and much evil may be anticipated." Approximately three thousand Cherokees attended the council. Ross used the occasion to speak out against the treaty and to harden the Cherokees against the idea of removal. Wool was later censured for allowing the council meeting.[3]

General Wool took it upon himself to issue food to the indigent Cherokees, then turned the responsibility over to the Indian commissioners. The commissioners requisitioned blankets and army rations from Wool for the Cherokees collecting at New Echota in preparation for enrollment and emigration.[4]

In October 1836, Wool wrote to Major General Alexander Macomb concerning his efforts to win the confidence of the Cherokees in order to get them to enroll voluntarily: "I have done everything in my power not only to conciliate the Cherokees, but to protect them in all the rights and privileges secured to them by the treaty. This they have no hesitation to acknowledge. Scarcely a day passes that some complaint is not made that a Cherokee has either lost a horse, a hog, or a cow, or his house or lands, which require my interference. I think I have restored four stolen horses within the last two weeks, and protected numbers in the possession of their houses, lands, and ferries. This, with the supplies which have been furnished in rations and clothing, has given me a claim to their confidence, and my decided course has commanded their respect and obedience."[5]

Although staunchly determined to carry out his duties as an officer of the army and to enforce the removal treaty, Wool became sympathetic to the Cherokees' situation. He professed that he would remove "every Indian tomorrow beyond the reach of the white men." He characterized the whites as vultures waiting to strip the Cherokees of everything they had and everything they were entitled to under the terms of the treaty.[6]

By the spring of 1837, enrollment and emigration had fallen far below the expectations of Wool and the Indian commissioners. He had been censured by Jackson for forwarding the Cherokees' protests to Washington and was being criticized by the governors of the various states involved, particularly Alabama, for undermining the removal effort. Wool requested a transfer from his Cherokee post. In May 1837, Colonel William Lindsay, arriving from recent duty in the Seminole War, replaced Wool in the Cherokee territory.[7]

Below is an appeal from Wool to the Cherokee people, pleading with them to enroll for emigration. He warns that if they don't take advantage of the beneficial provisions of the treaty, they will be captured and forced to emigrate and will lose their possessions without fair reimbursement.

Brigadier General John E. Wool's appeal to the Cherokees

Head Quarters, Army
Cherokee Nation, New Echota, Ga.
March 22nd, 1837

CHEROKEES:

It is nearly a year since I first arrived in this country. I then informed you of the objects of my coming among you. I told you that a treaty had been made with your people, and that your country was to be given up to the United States by the 25th May, 1838 a (little more than a year from this time,) when you would all be compelled to remove to the West. I also told you, if you would submit to the terms of the treaty I would protect you in your persons and property, at the same time I would furnish provisions and clothing to the poor and destitute of the Nation. You would not listen, but turned a deaf ear to my advice. You preferred the counsel of those who were opposed to the treaty. They told you, what was not true, that your people had made no treaty with the United States, and that you would be able to retain your lands, and would not be obliged to remove to the West, the place designated for your new homes. Be no longer deceived by such advice! It is not only untrue, but if listened to, may lead to your utter ruin. The President, as well as Congress, have decreed that you should remove from this country. The people of Georgia, of North Carolina, of Tennessee and of Alabama, have decreed it. Your fate is decided; and if you do not voluntarily get ready and go by the time fixed in the treaty, you will then be forced from this country by the soldiers of the United States.

Under such circumstances what will be your condition! Deplorable in the extreme! Instead of the benefits now presented to you by the treaty, of receiving pay for the improvements of your lands, your houses, your cornfields and your ferries, and for all the property unjustly taken from you by the white people, and at the same time, blankets, clothing and provisions for the poor, you will be driven from the country, and without a cent to support you on your arrival at your new homes. You will in vain flee to your mountains for protection. Like the Creeks, you will be hunted up and dragged from your lurking places and hurried to the West. I would ask, are you prepared for such scenes? I trust not. Yet such will be your fate if you persist in your present determination.

Cherokees: I have not come among you to oppress you, but to protect you and to see that justice is done you, as guarantied by the treaty. Be advised, and turn a deaf ear to those who would induce you to believe that no treaty has been made with you, and that you will not be obliged to leave your country. They cannot be friends, but the worst of enemies. Their advice, if followed, will lead to your certain destruction. The President has said that a treaty has been made with you, and must be executed agreeably to its terms. The President never changes.

Therefore, take my advice: It is the advice of a friend, who would tell you the truth and who feels deeply interested in your welfare, and do every thing in his power to relieve, protect and secure to you the benefits of the treaty. And why not abandon a country no longer yours? Do you not see the white people daily coming into it, driving you from your homes and possessing your houses, your cornfields and your ferries? Hitherto I have been able in some degree, to protect you from their intrusions; in a short time it will no longer be in my power. If, however, I could protect you, you could not live with them. Your habits, your manners and your customs are unlike, and unsuited to theirs. They have no feelings, no sympathies in common with yourselves. Leave then this country, which after the 25th May 1838, can afford you no protection, and remove to the country designated for your new homes, which is secured to you and your children forever; and where you may live under your own laws, and the customs of your fathers, without intrusion or molestation from the white man. It is a country much better than the one you now occupy; where you can grow more corn, and where game is more abundant. Think seriously of what I say to you! Remember that you have but one summer more to plant corn in this country. Make the best use of this time, and dispose of your property to the best advantage. Go and settle with the Commissioners, and with the emigrating Agent, Gen. Smith, receive the money due for your improvements, your houses, your cornfields and ferries, and for the property which has been unjustly taken from you by the whitemen, and at the appointed time be prepared to remove. In the mean time, if you will apply to me or my Agents, I will cause rations, blankets and clothing to be furnished to the poor and destitute of your people.

John E. Wool
Brig. Gen'l
Comdg.[8]

THE TALK
August 1837

IN THE SPRING OF 1837, John Ross went to Washington, D.C., and visited influential friends of the Cherokees to seek advice on how to overturn the 1835 Treaty of New Echota. He also published a pamphlet questioning the authority of the federal government to make treaties with a small faction of the tribe. After returning home to Red Hill in May, he called for a General Council of the Cherokees, to be held at the Red Clay Council Grounds beginning on July 31.

Federal officials then in the Cherokee Nation, including the new superintendent of Cherokee emigration, Colonel William Lindsay, were afraid that Ross's purposes in calling the council meeting were to protest the Treaty of New Echota and to encourage the Cherokees to stop emigration enrollment. Ross assured Lindsay that the meeting was not intended for any overt reason but to inform his people of the work of the Cherokee delegation that had just returned from Washington.

A week before the council meeting was to commence, Lindsay received permission to allow the meeting. He notified Ross, who seemed determined to proceed with the meeting with or without permission.[1]

The Red Clay Council Grounds were located in Tennessee just across the border from Georgia, inside the boundaries of the Cherokee Nation and outside the control of the Georgia government and the Georgia Guard. Though the Cherokees had held meetings there for a number of years, the council grounds increased in importance when many of the operations and meetings of the Cherokee Nation were moved there in 1832 due to the oppression of the Georgia government.

The General Council of 1837 drew an estimated three to four thousand Cherokees. Ross addressed the Cherokees about the delegation's visit to Washington as well as a trip he had taken to Arkansas. He described the lands set aside for them in the West as uninhabitable. Resolutions to condemn the Treaty of New Echota were made at the meeting. Additionally, a call to send a new delegation to Washington was made, contrary to Ross's promise to Lindsay for a noncontroversial meeting. A special emissary from the federal government, John Mason, Jr., spoke to the General Council on August 7 to encourage emigration. He gently reiterated the federal government's intention to enforce the removal treaty.[2]

Mason traveled from Gainesville, Georgia, to the Red Clay Council Grounds with an Englishman named George W. Featherstonhaugh. A naturalist and geologist on a long journey through North America, Featherstonhaugh later wrote a two-volume book on his travels. He met the missionaries at the Brainerd Mission and visited Spring Place before traveling to the Red Clay Council Grounds, where he enjoyed tea with Brigadier General Nathaniel Smith.

Below are excerpts from Featherstonhaugh's journal outlining some of the events at the Red Clay Council Grounds in

August 1837. He describes meeting several of the important leaders at the council, including John Mason, Colonel Lindsay, and John Ross. He also attends church services led by two of the most prominent missionaries in the Cherokee Nation. The Reverend Evan Jones, a Baptist missionary, was a staunch supporter of John Ross and later served as an assistant conductor for one of the emigration parties. The Reverend Jesse Bushyhead, one of the most respected Cherokee preachers, later served as a runner sent to the mountains to ask Cherokees to come out of hiding and join their countrymen in emigration. Bushyhead also led a detachment of emigrants in the winter of 1838-39 and had a daughter born just after crossing the Mississippi River.

After departing Red Clay, Featherstonhaugh resumed his travels by visiting several sites in northern Georgia on his way to South Carolina.

After the council ended, John Ross set out once again for Washington to lobby Congress to overturn the Treaty of New Echota.[3]

Excerpts from the journal of George W. Featherstonhaugh on the Cherokee General Council at Red Clay

August 5— . . . The expense of feeding this multitude, which was defrayed by the council, was very great. Fifteen beeves were said to be killed every day, and a proportionate quantity of Indian corn used. Twenty-four native families were employed in cooking the provisions and serving the tables which were set out three times a-day. The beef was cut up into small pieces of three or four inches square, and kept stewing for several hours in large pots. The broth of this mess, without the meat, was the first dish offered to us at the excellent Mrs. Walker's, but when it was handed to me I found it was nothing but a mass of melted fat, the surface of which was oscillating about like quicksilver, and I had to send it away at the risk of giving offence. It was a most amusing scene to walk from table to table and see the Cherokees eat; every one was permitted to eat as much as he pleased, just as at the Bodas of Camacho; it really appeared to me as if they never would be satisfied, and as if their real business was not to refresh themselves, but to gormandize every thing up that was set before them. Upon making further inquiries, I learnt that Mr. John Ross was the sole director of every thing, that he paid about three hundred dollars a day to the persons who contracted to furnish the provisions, the beef being paid for at the rate of four cents a pound. The expense was ultimately to be carried to account of the Cherokee fund. Mr. Ross invited us to dine with him at his house to-morrow.

In the evening the same scene of gormandizing was again exhibited, the woods gleaming with fires in every direction; several thousand Indians being scattered about in small groups, each with its fire, near to which a few sticks were set up, and a blanket or two laid over them to screen the women and children from the wind. The greatest tranquillity prevailed, and I walked about among them to a late hour, observing them, and asking the men the names of things with a view to catch the pronunciation.

August 6—Rising at day-break, and taking a cup of tea, I went to the Council-house to attend divine service. From a rostrum erected near it, a native Cherokee preacher delivered a very long sermon to a very numerous assemblage of Indians and white people who had assembled from various parts. The discourse came from him with great vehemence both of action and voice, gesticulating and grunting at every instant, and never stopping to take breath, as it appeared to me, in half an hour. It was like a continual stream of falling water. All the Cherokees paid great attention to the sermon, and the most perfect decorum prevailed. After the sermon we had a psalm, led by Bushy-head, the whole congregation uniting in it. Mr. Jones then preached in English, and Bushy-head, with his stentorian voice, translated the passages as they came from the preacher, into Cherokee. During all this time, the ardent beams of the sun were pouring upon our bare heads. I felt at length as if I could not bear it much longer, and therefore went away before we were dismissed, rather than by covering my head to appear to offer any irreverence.[4]

August 7—This was the day appointed for the delivery of the "Talk" or public address of Mr. Mason, the special agent, which was expected with great anxiety, and which Mr. Mason had been much occupied in the composition of. After breakfast, Foreman, the interpreter, came to the hut, and Mr. Mason gave him the "Talk" to study; he appeared to be a very intelligent man, and perfectly well acquainted with the English tongue. He told us some amusing anecdotes of an agent, named Schermerhorn, who had been appointed by the United States Government a year or two ago, as a commissioner to negotiate with the Cherokees. This man was a sort of loose Dutch Presbyterian Minister, and having taken up the calling of a political demagogue, had been rewarded with this situation by the President, Mr. Van Buren, a Dutchman also by birth. On coming amongst the Cherokees, instead of dealing fairly with them, and making an arrangement with the Council that could be sanctioned by a majority of the nation, he corrupted a few individuals to consent to emigrate, and deliver up the Cherokee territory; and reported it to the Government as if it had been a solemn contract entered into with the whole nation. The Reverend agent, also, being of amorous turn had been detected tampering with some of the young Cherokee women, so that he came to be an object of detestation to the Indians, who took every opportunity to affront him. Not more than half-a-dozen in the whole nation would speak to him at all; and whenever the rest of them met him, they made a point of turning round and presenting their backs to him. But this was not all the mortification his evil deeds brought upon him.

It is the custom of most of the Indian nations to give an Indian name to every white man who has any transactions with them of importance, or who has struck their fancy in any way. If the proper name of the individual corresponds in sound with any term in their language, they simply translate it. On the other hand, if they can find no equivalent in their own tongue, they look for words, which sound like the name they are unable to translate, and if those words are at all appropriate to the individual, whether in his appearance, his habits and customs, or character, they use them to form his Indian name. In doing this, they are remarkably skilful, and are as prompt and happy as the best *improvisatori* are in Italy. The name the Cherokees gave to me is an instance of this. It was found impossible to translate the word Featherstonhaugh, but one of their poets suggested that my Cherokee name should be Oóstanaúlee, which means "gravel or shingle brought down by floods." Having observed me frequently poking and hammering about in beds of gravel, the word which sounded something like my name, admirably answered the purpose. For the Rev. Mr. Schermerhorn, they had been so fortunate as to find a name that corresponded precisely to their estimate of him, and which was immediately adopted by the whole nation, especially the women and children, who were extremely tickled with it. It was Skáynooyáunah, or literally the "devil's horn." After I knew this story, I found it was only necessary to ask the women if they knew Skáynooyáunah to set them laughing.

August 7 [later]—The rain had been falling incessantly for thirty hours, and our hut being roofed with nothing but pine branches gave us very little protection; the bedclothes were wet through, and we were thoroughly nonplussed what to do. It was impossible to remain long in this state without becoming sick. The Indians, at the numerous bivouacs were all wet through, and apprehensions were beginning to be entertained by the Council, that a serious sickness might fall upon them if they were detained twenty-four hours more in the uncomfortable state they were in. The chiefs, therefore, were desirous that Mr. Mason should deliver his "Talk" immediately; but that gentleman, supposing the "Talk" would be deferred, was gone to Colonel Lindsay's for shelter. Mr. Ross therefore called upon me, and drew such a picture of the consequences that might ensue, that I wrote to Mr. Mason, and sent the note with a messenger. In this note, I related what Mr. Ross had said, and submitted to him, as the day had been appointed for the purpose, the propriety of being punctual, as want of punctuality would give the chiefs an opportunity of dismissing the nation and laying the blame upon him. The messenger returned about 3 P.M. with information to Mr. Ross that he might assemble the nation. Accordingly, horns were blown and public criers went into the woods to summon all the males to the Council-house; but recommending to the women and children to remain at their fires. Every one was now in motion, notwithstanding that the rain continued to fall in torrents.

At 4 P.M., Mr. Ross conducted Mr. Mason, Colonel Lindsay, Colonel Smith, and myself, into a stand erected near the Council-house, open at the sides, and from whence we could view an assemblage of about two thousand male Cherokees standing in the rain awaiting the "Talk" that was to be delivered. The special agent now advanced to the front of the stand, and read his address which was translated to them by the interpreter; after which, Mr. Gunter addressed them, requesting them to remain until the Council had taken the "Talk" into consideration, and informing them that plenty of provisions would continue to be provided for them, upon which they gave him a hearty grunt and dispersed. The scene was an imposing one; the Cherokees were attentive and behaved very well, but it was

no justice from whites

evident the "Talk" made no impression upon them. If the special agent had declared, in the name of his Government, that the Cherokee nation should continue to enjoy their native land, it would have been most enthusiastically received; but anything short of that was a proof to them that there was no hope left for justice from the whites, nor any resource for them but in the wisdom of their National Council. The "Talk" itself was full of friendly professions towards the nation, and dwelt upon the advantages it would derive from a peaceful compliance with the policy of the Government; but there was a passage in it which showed that the United States Government were determined to enforce the treaty which the minority had made with the Government, and even insinuated that the resistance to it was factious. This gave offence, and even Mr. Ross objected to it.

The Government now could only carry its policy out by gaining the chiefs, or by military force. From what I observed, the chiefs, if not incorruptible, were determined not to come to terms without securing great advantages, whilst it was their intention not to precipitate things, but to gain time and make another appeal to the Congress. Many of them who had heard of me through Mr. Buttrick, and who saw the interest I took in their affairs and in acquiring some knowledge of their language, spoke to me on the subject; but I invariably advised them to submit to the Government, for a successful resistance was impossible. I gave it also as my opinion that it was a very possible thing that if they procrastinated, a collision would soon take place betwixt them and the Georgians and Tennesseans, which would involve the destruction of the nation. These opinions, it was evident to me, were very unwelcome to them; and after the delivery of the "Talk," I declined saying anything on the subject. The rain continued to pour down, and on reaching my quarters, I found the hut a perfect swamp, and full of people all wet through, as many as could get there sitting on my bed. A more uncomfortable place I certainly never was in; everything was wet and smelt ill. All I could do was to lie down upon the wet bed, and keep the crowd off with my feet and arms. It was late in the night before we got rid of them: the rain still coming down in torrents.

August 8—I rose at the dawn of day to witness a thick, close atmosphere, with the rain pouring down harder than ever. It was quite impossible that matters should remain in this state long: the low ground upon which the Council had assembled the nation would soon be entirely covered with water as well as the floor of my hut, for it was mine now, the special agent having changed his quarters to Colonel Lindsay's: all amateurs being left to shift for themselves. I therefore wrote to Colonel Lindsay, stating my disagreeable situation, and asked if he would put me in a way to return to Spring Place. In the meantime, Mr. Bushy-head sent for me to breakfast with his family, and meet some old chiefs of whom I wished to ask some questions respecting some of their most authentic traditions, as well as to read over some of my vocabularies to them for the correction of the pronunciation. From thence I had determined, in the event of Colonel Lindsay not being able to assist me, to walk in the rain to the Missionary establishment, as I began to feel a sick head-ache and pains in my limbs which would probably end in a fever. At any rate, I had determined to abandon the hut.

Whilst I was pondering over my situation, Colonel Lindsay, to my great joy, sent me a capital saddle-horse, with a well-mounted dragoon to attend me. I now bustled about, took leave of the chiefs, and giving the reins to my steed, took to the woods again. Although the rain beat furiously in my face, I could not keep my eyes off the many hundreds of poor Cherokee families cowering with their children under their little blanket tents, all wet through; the men protecting them from the weather as well as they could, and keeping their fires alive with great difficulty. It was a very curious spectacle.[5]

Too Sick to Travel

October–December 1837

CAPTAIN B. B. CANNON'S First Regiment of Tennessee Volunteer Infantry was mustered in for service for the Cherokee War at Dallas in Hamilton County, Tennessee, on June 27, 1837. The Tennessee Volunteers signed up for twelve months of service.[1]

Between June and October 1837, there was not much action for Cannon's men. Most of the military stationed in Cherokee country were there as a precaution, should wide-scale violence break out, which it never did, and to assist enrolling agents and subsistence officers in providing food and supplies to Cherokees who came in to voluntarily enroll for emigration.

In October, Captain Cannon was assigned to lead a detachment of 365 Cherokees from Charleston, Tennessee, on an overland route to the new Cherokee lands set aside in the West. Captain Cannon's detachment was the first to follow the northern route through Tennessee, Kentucky, Illinois, Missouri, and Arkansas. Most of the John Ross-managed land detachments would take the same route the next year.[2]

Cannon's land detachment and those that followed used established roads, many of which are no longer in use today. Those roads passed through towns and near documented springs and other sources of water. The detachments needed access to towns for supplies and repairs, and they required sites near water for encampments. The area near what is now Reelfoot Lake in northeastern Tennessee and the New Madrid fault was avoided because of the terrifying earthquakes of 1811-12, which resulted in the creation of the lake. The earthquake drove many settlers away from the area and damaged roads. Parts of southeastern Missouri were avoided because of swamps and lack of settlements. Cannon's party and many later detachments took a more northerly route, crossing the Mississippi River near Cape Girardeau, Missouri.[3]

The Cannon detachment was a government-financed group of Treaty Party sympathizers. The Cherokee leader of the group was James Starr, and the interpreter was Charles Reese. Reese and Starr stopped in Nashville on their journey west to visit former president Andrew Jackson.

Along the way, the Cannon detachment was overtaken by other parties who wanted to travel with the group. These included Richard Timberlake, George Ross, and Isaac Walker. Dr. Grandville and Dr. G. S. Townsend were two physicians who accompanied the party.[4]

Below is Captain B. B. Cannon's journal of the emigration. Townsend's record of the trip is presented in the next chapter. The party had to stop for several days due to the severe illness of many members. Fifteen deaths were reported by Dr. Townsend before the Cherokees in the detachment were turned over to Lieutenant Van Horne in the western territories on December 30, 1837.

Captain B. B. Cannon's journal of a land detachment

October 13th 1837—Sent the waggons to the Indian encampment [at Charleston, Tennessee] and comenced loading in the evening.

October 14th 1837—Completed loading the waggons and crossed the Heighwassie [Hiwassee] river at Calhoun, encamped on the North bank of Highwassee at 5:00 P.M.

October 15th 1837—Marched the Party at 8 oc. [o'clock] A.M., halted & encamped at Spring Creek at 11 oc. A.M. where Genl Smith mustered the Party which consumed the remainder of the day. 5 miles to day.

October 16th 1837—Marched at 800 A.M., halted & encamped at Kelley's ferry on the Tennessee river at 400 P.M., issued corn & fodder, corn meal and bacon. Made 14 miles to day.

Oct 17th 1837—Commenced ferrying the Tennessee at 8 oc. A.M. having been detained until the sun dispelled the fog, every thing being in readiness to commence at day light, completed ferrying the Party at 4 oc. P.M. and reached Little Richland Creek at 8 oc. to where the Party had been directed to halt and encamp, issued corn & fodder. 7 miles.

Oct 18th 1837—Marched at ½ past 7 oc. A.M. One of the Provision Waggons oversat [overturned], which detained a half hour, no damage done, ascended Wallens [Walden's] Ridge (the ascent 2 miles) halted at Ragsdales, 5 miles in all. at 1½ oc. P.M. encamped and issued corn fodder and corn meal & bacon. All wearied getting up the mountain and 10 miles further to water.

Oct 19th 1837—Marched at ½ after 7 oc. A.M., descended

the mountain, and encamped at Sequachee [Sequatchie] river near Mr. Springs at 2:00 P.M. 11½ miles, issued corn & fodder all in good order.

Oct 20th 1837—Marched at ½ after 6 oc. A.M. ascended Cumberland Mountain, arrived at Mr. Flemings at ¾ after 3 oc P.[M.] encamped and issued corn & fodder, corn meal & Bacon. Water very scarce, 14½ miles to day.

Oct 21st 1837—Marched at ½ after 7 oc. A.M. descended the mountain and arrived at Collins river ¼ after 4 oc. P.M. encamped and issued corn & fodder—The Indians appear fatigued this evening—made 13 miles to day road extremely rough.

Oct 22nd 1837—Marched at 8 oc. A.M. arrived at Mr. Britts at ½ after 12 oc. P.M. encamped & issued corn & fodder, corn meal & Bacon made 7½ miles to day. Passed through McMinnville, o[b]tained a quantity of corn meal & Bacon, at McMinnville—no water for 12 miles ahead.

Oct 23rd 1837—Marched at ½ after 6 oc. A.M. Capt. Prigmore badly hurt by a waggon horse, attempting to run away—arrived at a creek near Woodbury, at ½ after 4 oc. P.M. encamped and issued corn & fodder, made 20 miles to day.

Oct 24th 1837—Marched at ½ after 7 oc. A.M. arrived at Mr. Yearwoods at 4 oc. P.M. rained last night and to day. made 15 miles. Issued corn & fodder, cornmeal and Bacon.

Oct 25th 1837—Marched at 800 buried Andrews child at 9½ oc. A.M. Passed through Murfreesborugh [Murfreesboro, Tennessee] and arrived at Overalls Creek 4 oc. P.M. 14 miles to day. Issued corn & fodder.

Oct 26th 1837—Marched at 8 oc A.M. passed through three Turnpike gates. arrived at Mr. Harris—at 3 oc. P.M. encamped and issued corn-meal & Bacon, corn & fodder, made 16½ miles to day.

Oct 27th 1837—Marched at ½ after 7 oc. A.M. passed through 2 turnpike gates. Nashville and across the Cumberland river on the Nashville toll bridge, arrived at Mr. Putnams ½ after 300 P.M. encamped and issued corn & fodder. Isaac Walker, an emigrant overtook us. Mr. L. A. Kincannon, contracting agent, left us and returned home, having, on the way, near McMinnville, signified his intentions *verbally* to do so, assigning as the reason the delicate situation of his health. 13 miles to day.

Oct 28th 1837—Rested for the purpose of washing clothes repairing waggons, and horse shoeing—Reese, Starr, and others of the emigrants, visited Genl Jackson who was at Nashville, Issued corn & fodder, corn meal & Bacon. Assigned Mr. E. S. Curry to supply the place of Kincannon.

Oct 29th 1837—Marched at ½ after 8 oc. A.M. Halted at Long Creek at ½ after 2 oc. P.M. encamped & issued corn & fodder, made 13½ miles to day.

Oct 30th 1837—Marched at ½ after 7 oc. A.M. arrived at & forded Little Red river. at ½ after 5 oc. P.M. encamped and issued corn meal & Bacon, corn & fodder, made 18½ miles to day.

Oct 31st 1837—Marched at 8 oc. A.M. arrived at Mr. Graves, Kentucky at 300 P.M. Issued corn & fodder, made 16 miles.

Nov 1st 1837—Marched at 8 oc. A.M. buried Ducks child this morning. passed through Hopkinsville Ken[tucky] and arrived at Mr. Northerns at ½ after 500 P.M. Issued corn & fodder, flour & Bacon. made 19 miles to day.

Nov 2nd 1837—Marched at 8 oc. A.M. and at 300 P.M. arrived one mile in advance of Mr. Mitcherson. Issued corn & fodder, made 13 miles to day.

Nov 3rd 1837—David Simpson and Pheasant, Emigrants, came up last night, and joined the party, having been heretofore enrolled and mustered. Marched at 8 oc. A.M. passed through Princeton Ken. halted and encamped near Mr. Barnetts at ½ after 6 oc. P.M. Issued corn & fodder, Flour & Bacon, made 17 miles to day.

Nov 4th 1837—Marched at 8 oc. A.M. passed through Fredonia Ken encamped at Threlkelds branch at 4 oc. P.M. Issued corn & fodder, made 15 miles to day.

Nov. 5th 1837—Marched at 8 oc. A.M. passed through Salem, halted and encamped at another Mr. Threlkelds branch, at 4 oc. P.M. Issued corn & fodder, corn meal & Bacon, and a small quantity of flour. 13½ miles to day.

Nov 6th 1837—Marched at 7 oc. A.M. arrived at Berry's ferry (Golconda opposite on the Ohio river) at 9 oc. A.M. everything in readiness to commence ferrying but prevented on account of the extreme roughness of the river, produced by high winds—which continued the remainder of the day—encamped in good order & issued corn & fodder. 5½ miles to day.

Nov 7th 1837—Commenced ferrying at ½ after 5 oc. A.M. moved the Party one mile as it crossed and encamped completed crossing at 4 oc. P.M. all safely. Issued corn & fodder, corn meal & Bacon. 1 mile to day.

Nov 8th 1837—Marched at 8 oc. A.M. Mr. Reese & myself remained behind and buried a child of Seabolts. Overtook the party, halted and encamped at Big bay Creek at 4 oc. P.M. Issued corn & fodder. James Starr & his wife left this morning with two carryalls to take care of three of their sons who were too sick to travel, with instructions to overtake the Party as soon as possible without endangering the lives of his children. 15 miles to day.

Nov 9th 1837—Marched at 8 oc. A.M. halted and encamped at Cash Creek ½ past 4 oc. P.M. Issued Corn & fodder, corn meal & Bacon. 15 miles to day.

Nov 10th 1837—Marched at 8 oc. A.M. were detain[ed] on the way 2 hours making a bridge across a small creek, halted at Cypress creek. 4 oc. P.M. encamped and issued corn & fodder and salt. 14 miles to day.

Nov 11th 1837—Marched at 8 oc. A.M. passed thro' Jonesborough, Ill., halted and encamped at Clear creek in the Mississippi bottom. Issued corn & fodder, corn meal & Bacon. 13 miles to day.

Nov 12th 1837—Marched at 8 oc. A.M. arrived at the Mississippi River at 10 oc. A.M. Commence ferrying at 11 oc. directed the party to move a short distance as they crossed the river & encamp. Issued corn & fodder, suspended crossing at 500 P.M. encamped near the ferry landing. 5 miles to day. Starr came up, Richd Timberlake & George Ross overtook and enrolled.

Nov 13th 1837—Continued ferrying from 7 oc. until 10 oc. A.M. when the wind arose and checked our progress. 3 oc. P.M. resumed and made one trip, suspended at 5 oc. P.M. Issued corn & fodder, corn-meal & Bacon. [B]uried Ducks child.

Nov 14th 1837—Crossed the remainder of the Party,

marched at 10 oc. A.M. arrived, at Williams, encamped & issued corn & fodder. Sickness prevailing. 5 miles to day.

Nov 15th 1837—Rested for the purpose of Washing. Issued corn & fodder, corn meal & Bacon.

Nov 16th 1837—Marched at 8 oc. A.M. left Reese & Starr and families on account of sickness in their families, also James Taylor (Reese's son in law) and family. Taylor himself being very sick, with Instructions to overtake the Party if possible— passed through Jackson Mo. halted and encamped at Widow Roberts on the road via Farmington. Issued corn only no fodder to be had. 17 miles to day.

Nov 17th 1837—Marched at 8 oc. A.M. halted at Whitewater creek at 4 oc. Issued corn & fodder, corn meal and beef. 13 miles to day.

Nov 18th 1837—Received a quantity of flour this morning, marched at 8 o'c A.M. halted at Morands at 5 o'c P.M.— encamped and issued flour & Bacon. 16 miles to day.

Nov 19th 1837—Marched at 8 o'c A.M. took in a quantity of Beef, Bacon & cornmeal. halted and encamped at ½ past 4 o'c P.M. Issued corn & fodder at Wolf creek. 14 miles to day.

Nov 20th 1837—Marched at 8 o'c A.M. passed through Farmington, Mo. took in a barrel of salt. halted at St. Francis river at 4 o'c P.M. encamped and issued 2 rations Flour & 1 of beef—corn & fodder. 15 miles to day.

Nov 21st 1837—A considerable number drunk last night obtained the liquor at Farmington, had to get out of bed about midnight to quell the disorder, a refusal by several to march this morning, alleging that they would wait for Starr & Reese, to come up at that place, Marched at 8 o'c in defiance of threats and attempts to intimidate, none remained behind passed through Caledonia, halted at Mr. Jacksons, at 4 o'c P.M. encamped & Issued one days rations beef & Bacon (mostly bacon). Issued corn & fodder. 14 miles to day.

Nov 22nd 1837—Marched at ½ after 8 o'c A.M. passed the Leadmines (or Courtois diggings) [Washington County, Missouri] arrived at Scotts 4 o'c P.M. Issued corn & fodder and cornmeal. 13 miles to day.

Nov 23rd 1837—Rested for the purpose of repairing waggons, Schoeing horses, washing &c. Starr, Reese, & Taylor came up, the health of their families in some degree improved. Issued corn & fodder, beef. Weather very cold.

Nov 24th 1837—Marched half after 8 o'c considerable sickness prevailing, arrived at Huzza Creek [Crawford County], 4 o'c P.M. encamped and issued corn & fodder, 12 miles to day.

Nov 25th 1837—Doct. Townsend officially advised a suspension of our march, in consequence of the severe indisposition of several families, for a time sufficient for the employment of such remedial agents as their respective cases might require. I accordingly directed the Party to remain in camp, and make the best possible arrangements for the sick. In the evening issued corn & fodder, Flour & beef, for 1 day.

Nov 26th 1837—Remained in camp sickness continuing, in the evening issued beef & cornmeal, for 1 day, and corn & fodder.

Nov 27th 1837—Remained in camp, sickness continuing,

in the evening issued corn & fodder, Bacon & corn meal.

Nov 28th 1837—Moved the detachment 2 miles further to a spring and School house, obtained permission for as many of the sick to occupy the school house as could do so, a much better situation for an encampment than on the creek, sickness increasing. Issued corn & fodder.

Nov 29th 1837—Remained in camp, sickness increasing. Issued corn and fodder, buried Corn Tassel's child to day.

Nov 30th 1837—Remained in camp, sickness continuing. Issued corn & fodder.

Decr 1st 1837—Remained in camp, sickness abating. Issued corn & fodder, Bacon & corn meal, buried Oolanheta's child to day.

Decr 2nd 1837—Remained in camp, sickness abating. Issued beef and corn meal, corn & fodder.

Decr 3rd 1837—Remained in camp, sickness abating. Issued corn & fodder.

Decr 4th 1837—Marched at 9 o'c A.M. buried George Killion and left Mr. Wells to bury a waggoner (black boy) who died this morning. Scarcely room in the waggons for the sick, halted the party at Mr. Davis 4½ oc. P.M. had to move down the creek a mile off the road to get wood. Issued corn & fodder and corn meal for 1 day. 11 miles to day.

Decr 5th 1837—Marched at 9 o'c A.M. Two waggoners left (black boys) sick this morning. halted at Merrimac river at ½ after 3 o'c P.M. encamped and Issued corn & fodder, cornmeal & beef. 10 miles to day.

Decr 6th 1837—Marched at 9 o'c A.M. passed Masseys Iron Works [Meramac Spring Park near St. James, Missouri], halted at Mr. Jones ½ after 3 o'c P.M. Encamped and Issued corn & fodder, 12 miles to day.

Decr 7th 1837—March at ½ after 8 o'c A.M. halted at Mr. Bates at 5 o'c P.M. encamped and issued corn & fodder corn meal and Bacon. Reese's team ran away—broke his waggon and Starrs carry-all, left him and family about 3 miles back to get his waggon mended, to overtake as soon as possible. 20 miles to day.

Decr 8th 1837—Buried Nancy Bigbears Grand child. Marched at 9 o'c A.M. halted at Piney river, ½ after 3 o'c P.M. rained all day, encamped and issued corn only—no fodder to be had, several drunk, 11 miles to day.

Decr 9th 1837—Marched at 9 o'c A.M. Mayfields waggon broke down at about a mile, left him to get it mended and to overtake, halted at Waynesville, Mo. 4 o'c P.M. encamped and issued corn & fodder, Beef & cornmeal, several drunk, extremely cold. 12½ miles to day.

Decr 10th 1837—Marched at 8 oc. A.M. halted at the Gasconade river 4 o'c P.M. Issued corn & fodder. 14 miles to day.

Decr 11th 1837—Marched at ½ after 8 o'c A.M. halted at Sumners, 4 oc. encamped and issued corn & fodder, 15 miles to day.

Decr 12th 1837—Marched at 9 o'c A.M. halted one mile in advance of Mr. Parkes at a branch, 4 o'c P.M. encamped and issued corn & fodder, beef, some bacon & corn meal. 14 miles to day.

Decr 13th 1837—Marched at ½ after 8 o'c A.M. halted at a branch near Mr. Eddingtons. 4 o'c P.M. encamped and issued corn & fodder, Reese & Mayfield came up. 13½ miles to day.

Decr 14th 1837—Marched at 8 o'c A.M. halted at James fork White river, near the road, but which does not cross the road. 3 o'c P.M. Mr Wells taken sick, issued corn meal, corn & fodder. 15½ miles to day.

Decr 15th 1837—Joseph Starrs wife had a boy child last night. Marched at ½ after 8 o'c A.M. halted at Mr. Danforths, 2 o'c P.M. waggoners having horses shod until late at night. Issued corn & fodder & beef. 10½ miles to day.

Decr 16th 1837—Issued Sugar & coffee to the Waggoners this morning. Marched at 9 o'c A.M. passed thro' Springfield, Mo. halted at 4 o'c P.M. encamped near Mr Clicks. Issued corn & fodder and corn meal. 12 miles to day.

Decr 17th 1837—Snowed last night. Buried Elleges wife, and Charles Timberlakes son, Smoker. Marched at 9 o'c A.M. halted at Mr. Dyes. 3 o'c, extremely cold, sickness prevailing to a considerable extent. all very much fatigued, encamped issued corn & fodder, and beef. 10 miles to day.

Decr 18th 1837—Detained to day on account [of sickness. Dr.] Townsend sent back to Springfield for medicines. Buried Dreadful Waters this evening—issued corn & fodder, and corn meal.

Decr 19th 1837—Detained to day also, on account of sickness—cold intense, Issued beef, corn & fodder.

Decr 20th 1837—Marched at ½ after 8 oc. A.M. Halted at

½ after 3 oc. P.M. at Mr Allens. encamped and issued corn & fodder and corn meal, 15 miles to day.

Decr 21st 1837—Marched at 8 oc. A.M. halted at Lockes, on Flat creek 3½ oc. P.M. encamped and Issued beef, corn & fodder, 15 miles to day.

Decr 22nd 1837—Burried Goddards Grand child, Marched at 8 oc. A.M. halted at McMurtrees. 3 o'c P.M., encamped and issued corn meal, corn & fodder, 15 miles to day.

Decr 23rd 1837—Buried Rainfrogs, or Lucy Redsticks daughter. Marched at 8 o'c A.M. halted at Reddicks 3 oc. P.M. encamped and Issued Beef, corn & fodder, 16 miles to day.

Decr 24th 1837—Marched at 8 oc. A.M. halted at the X Hollows—had to leave the Road ¾ mile to get water, at 3 o'c P.M. Issued corn & fodder, Pork & corn meal, 15 miles to day.

Decr 25th 1837—Marched at 8 oc. A.M. Took the right hand r[oad] to [Cane] Hill. at FitzGeralds, halted, and encamped [a ha]lf mile in advance of Mr. Cunninghams at a branch, 3 oc. P.M. Issued corn & fodder, & salt Pork. 15½ miles to day.

Decr 26th 1837—Marched at 8 oc. A.M. halted at James Coulters on Cane Hill, Ark, 3½ oc. P.M. Encamped and issued corn meal, corn & fodder, 16½ miles to day.

Decr 27th 1837—Buried Alsey Timberlakes Daughter of Charles Timberlake, Marched at 8 oc. A.M. halted at Mr. Beans in the Cherokee Nation West, at ½ past 2 oc. P.M. encamped and Issued corn and fodder, Fresh Pork & some beef. 12 miles to day.

Decr 28th 1837—The Party refused to go further, but at the same time pledged themselves to remain together until a remuster was made by the proper Officer—for whom I immediately sent an Express to Fort Gibson alleging that their refusal was in consequence of their sickness now prevailing—Doct. Reynolds the Disb[urs]ing Agent for the party Dismissed the Waggons from further service—buried another child of Chas Timberlakes—and one which was born (untimely) yesterday—of which no other account than this is taken. [Issued pork, cornmeal, and bacon. Lieutenant Van] Horne arrived late in the evening [having] missed my express on the way. Jesse [Halfbreed had] a child born last night.

Decr 29th 1837—Remustered the Party. Issued a small Quant[it]y of corn meal & Pork yet on hands.

Decr 30th 1837—Completed the Rolls of Remuster—turned over the party to Lieut Van Horne. Dismissed my Assistants.

Respectfully submitted
B. B. Cannon[5]

A DISTANCE SHORT
OF 800 MILES
January 1838

DR. G. S. TOWNSEND was one of two attending physicians for the Starr/Cannon detachment of 365 Cherokees. The detachment emigrated from Charleston, Tennessee, in mid-October 1837 and arrived in Indian territory in late December. Townsend kept detailed records of the medicines and hospital supplies he purchased for the emigrating party, as well as the number and causes of deaths along the way. At the end of the journey, he filed a report with C. A. Harris of the Bureau of Indian Affairs describing his experiences on the trip.[1]

Townsend kept a well-stocked supply of medicines and hospital articles to attend his patients. Among the many things he stocked were castor oil, magnesia, cayenne pepper, cream of tartar, extract of liquorice, ammonia water, anti-bilious pills, Epsom salts, essence of peppermint, alum, borat soda, pulverized rhubarb, gum opium, laudanum, Rio coffee, brown sugar, imperial tea, rice, whiskey, cognac, bicarbonate of potassium, camphor, nitre, elixir of vitriol, spirits of turpentine, wormseed oil, shake root, calomel, mustard, mercurial ointment, sulphur quinine, and syrup made from squills, a bulbous member of the lily family. His hospital equipment included thumb lancets, male and female syringes, apothecary scales and weights, pillboxes, vials, tin cups, tin buckets, and a medicine sock. Dr. Townsend also had use of a large, walled tent and a common tent for his hospital, both of which he turned over at the end of the trip to Dr. J. W. Lide, the director of medicine for Cherokee emigration.[2]

Dr. Townsend took an active interest in the health of his patients. When the emigration party became too ill to move, he spoke with the conductor, B. B. Cannon, to request a halt. He also asked that tents be supplied for the emigrating party. He was clearly frustrated when patients didn't take his advice on what to eat and when they declined the medicines he prescribed.

Townsend attached an "Abstract of the Number of Deaths" to his report. There, he listed the deaths of eleven children and four adults. Five children age two or under died of *cholera infantum*. One infant died of convulsions, and two died of "yaws," which may have involved some form of spasms or convulsions. Three older children died of dysentery. Two adults died of typhus fever and two of inflammation of the lungs.

Dr. Townsend remarked that one of the children who died of dysentery was "killed by the use of astringent Roots." It's not clear if this was something he prescribed or something that was recommended by a Cherokee medicine man. Regarding an adult, age sixty-five, who died of typhus fever, Townsend noted that the "disease [was] brought on by excessive fatigue and exposure from hunting" and that the victim "would not take medicine."

Below is Dr. Townsend's report. That report and information on other emigrating detachments make it clear that children and the elderly suffered the most. While the mortality rate for Dr. Townsend's detachment was high—approximately 4 percent—

it would prove lower than that for most of the succeeding detachments that followed the northern route.[3]

Dr. G. S. Townsend's report of a land detachment

Cherokee Agency East
January 25th 1838

Hon C. A. Harris,
Sir,

I have the honor to report my return here, on the 23d Inst. [instant—i.e., the present month] from the Cherokee Nation West, which place I left on the 31st Decr. having accompanied a Detachment of Cherokees, on their emigration thither, as attending Physician.

In the absence of any special instructions, as to the manner of making a report to the department, I shall briefly detail the events of the Journey, as connected with my official duties. The detachment left the Agency, in general good health, the only cases of disease were confined to six or seven children, who had been labouring for several months, under Cholera Infantum, and whose emaciated appearance gave but little hopes of recovery. The weather altho' at the middle of October, remain[ed] warm and dry and continued so untill after our arrival at the Ohio River, at which place we were detained for two days, in consequence of high winds. Whilst here four cases of fever, of a violent and malignant character, occured in the family of Mr. Starr, all of whom eventually recovered. On our arrival at the Mississippi, we were also detained two days, in crossing, and the emigrants, necessarily exposed to the miasmatic exhalations of the immense swamp, which skirted the shores of the River, the deleterious effects of which soon became manifest by the demands made for my services. The detachment continued its progress untill 25th November, when I found the increasing number of cases, rendered it absolutely necessary for the detachment to discontinue its march, in order that I might have some chance to combat with the formidable and overwhelming diseases that seemed to threaten the party with destruction.

I accordingly addressed a note to the Conducting Agent, giving my views of the subject. He did not hesitate to acceed to my proposal, for indeed the wagons, would have been unable to have hauled the sick, as many as 60 at that time being dangerously ill and could not bear transportation. Ten days elapsed before I felt myself authorised to pronounce their removal free from danger, and even then, cases were daily occuring, untill two thirds of the whole party had passed through the pestilence. Nor was the disease confined exclusively to the emigrants, nearly all the Drivers were sick, some of whom had to be left on the Road, and substitutes hired. We finaly arrived at our place of destination on the 29th of December without further detentions.

The causes which operated in producing the great amount of sickness as above stated were mainly attributeable to the unwholesome stagnant water which we were compelled to use throughout Illinois, the exposure to marsh effluvia, and the freedom with which the emigrants indulged in the use of fruits of every description, more particularly Grapes which proved a certain prelude to violent attacks of Dysentery and Bowel complaints, of a dangerous character.

Before setting out on the Journey, my opinion was asked by the Superintendent, as to the necessity of furnishing the emigrants with temporary Tent Cloths as a protection from the vicissitudes of the weather. And I unhesitatingly gave my opinion in favour of allowing them such protection. And I now feel much gratification in being able to state that without them a much greater amount of suffering would have been experienced and the human policy of the Government, frustrated by the utter inutility of medical prescriptions, where the patient was exposed to all the changes of weather incident to so long a journey.

I cannot refrain on this occasion, from obtruding my opinion on the attention of the department that the experiment just made of land transportation will not justify a repitition, either on account of economy, expedition or comfort to the Emigrants. The past Autumn has been one of uncommon mildness and the condition of the Roads, perhaps never excelled, yet with all this expedition compatible with the safety of the party near 80 days have been consumed in traversing a distance short of 800 miles. If I may be permitted to offer a suggestion on the subject, I should say that a much more expeditious and infinitely cheaper mode would be to convey the parties by water, either up the Arkansas or Missouri Rivers (as the state of the water would permit) to the nearest point of the Cherokee line, thence, transported in teams drawn by Oxen, which would find ample subsistance on the extensive Praires of this country without cost. The most eligable point of the country seems to me to be Booneville in Missouri as there is but little if any difficulty in ascending the River, to that place at any period, and a glance at the Map will show that the distance from thence to the Nation, will fall short of 200 miles. [B]ut of this the Department will be fully able to judge and I beg to be forgiven if my suggestions should appear irrelevant.

Enclosed I have forwarded an abstract of the number of deaths, which occured with their ages and diseases and beg in conclusion to state that I had to encounter great difficulties from the prejudices of some of the party about taking medicine and of the four adult deaths, three absolutely refused to take any, and persisted in their determination untill death colored the senses.

I have the honor to remain
Your most obt Servt

G. S. Townsend
attending Physicians to Emigrating Cherokee[4]

UNDER WEIGH AT DAYLIGHT

June 1838

WHEN THE DEADLINE for voluntary enrollment and removal passed on May 23, 1838, General Winfield Scott issued orders for mandatory collection to begin. The roundup started in Georgia. Most of the Georgia Cherokees and many Creek Indians who had been hiding in Cherokee country were brought to Ross's Landing via the Rossville and Brainerd Roads and down what is now Market Street in Chattanooga. Although Cherokees were also brought to Gunter's Landing and the Cherokee Agency at Charleston, Tennessee, no detachments left from those depots before the temporary cessation of emigration for the summer. In fact, no detachments of Cherokees are known to have left from Gunter's Landing, although one land detachment originating from the Fort Payne-Rawlingsville area and several water detachments passed through Gunter's Landing.[1]

The first detachment of Cherokees to leave by force

departed on June 6. It was under the command of Lieutenant Edward Deas. Deas was an experienced emigration conductor, having led a detachment of 250 volunteer Cherokees in April. He had also been involved in the removal of the Creeks as an enrolling agent and detachment leader in searching for Creeks hiding in Cherokee territory. The April detachment had left from Ross's Landing. Deas took command when it reached Waterloo, Alabama. That emigrating party traveled by steamboat and railroad. No deaths were reported on either the April detachment or the June detachment led by Deas.[2]

Most of the Cherokees and Creeks in Deas's June detachment were from Georgia. On June 9, Brigadier General Charles Floyd prepared a list of Indians sent to Ross's Landing from the Middle District. The list noted 334 Indians from Fort Gilmer, 469 from Fort Cumming, 122 from Spring Place, 950 from the Sixes, 467 from Fort Means, 225 from Fort Campbell, 198 from New Echota, and 479 from Fort Buffington—all in Georgia—and an additional 152 under escort of Captain Patton from an unlisted fort. By June 9, another 400 Cherokees were in the possession of the Georgia troops. In a report dated June 21, Colonel William Lindsay reported to General Scott that "of all the Indians who have been and are now at Ross's Landing 3,860 are from Georgia and 940 are from Tennessee."[3]

The first group of Cherokees was forced at gunpoint on to a steamboat and six flatboats at Ross's Landing. The steamboat was ironically named the *George Guess*, after the great Sequoyah, who invented the Cherokee syllabary and brought a high rate of literacy to the Cherokee Nation in just a few years. The Cherokees traveled by water to Decatur, Alabama, where they boarded trains to Tuscumbia, Alabama. From Tuscumbia, they went by steamboat to Waterloo, Alabama, in two groups. In Waterloo, the groups reunited aboard the steamboat *Smelter* and traveled north on the Tennessee River to Paducah, Kentucky. At Paducah, they entered the Ohio River and followed it west to the Mississippi. The water route then took them south on the Mississippi past Memphis, then along the White River to the Arkansas River. Their route then went northwest through Arkansas past Little Rock, the Lewisburg sand bar, and Fort Smith to Fort Coffee. Their intended destination was Fort Gibson in the heart of the Cherokee lands, but they chose to stop at Fort Coffee, about ten miles upstream of Fort Smith.[4]

Crowded on boats for most of the trip, the Cherokees were exposed to the elements. The assistant conductors and physicians were afforded more comfortable accommodations in the main cabins of the steamboat and had to pay separate fares. Passage on the *George Guess* was $5.00 for each of the conductors and $5.75 for physician Alfred M. Folger. Passage on the railroad from Decatur to Tuscumbia was $2.00. Passage on the *Smelter* to Fort Coffee was $65.00. Several detachment leaders also turned in miscellaneous bills, including tavern tabs at Ross's Landing and Tuscumbia Landing, dinners for $.25 or $.50 each, and washing expenses.[5]

The last of the pro-treaty detachments escorted by Deas left Charleston on October 11 and traveled to Ross's Landing, where it crossed the Tennessee River. Once across, the Cherokees camped on October 17 and 18 at what is now Coolidge Park in North Chattanooga while they waited for their absent conductor, John Adair Bell. Upon resuming, they walked across Moccasin Bend to Brown's Ferry and across Tennessee to Memphis, then overland to Little Rock and on to Oklahoma, arriving on January 7, 1839. Twenty-three deaths were reported out of 660 emigrants. Deas referred to the Bell detachment as the "so-called treaty" party," possibly because Bell and some of the others were supporters of the Treaty of New Echota. Surviving reports and vouchers for this detachment reveal that it had a considerable number of destitute Cherokees, who received purchases from a special "poor fund." Among the supplies Deas purchased for the poorer members of the detachment were blankets and shoes. He also purchased over 146 pounds of soap.[6]

Expense receipts kept by Deas included one for $51.00 to Benjamin Ragsdale "for furnishing materials and making 17 coffins for the dead of a Party of Cherokees, on the route of emigration, at sundry times from the 11 Oct. to the 1 Dec . . . and for assisting in digging graves and burying the dead at $3 for each coffin." A second receipt signed by Ragsdale and Deas was for $9.00 for three more coffins between December 7 and December 31. Between November 9 and November 11, Deas reimbursed Archibald Campbell $7.50 "for the hire of 2 horses and his services 3 days, returning from the main Party to bring up 3 sick Cherokees left on that account & burying two infants at $2.50 per day." This was early in their journey, while the party was still in Tennessee.[7]

Deas kept journals of his three trips escorting Cherokee detachments. The journals for his first two trips survive, but the third is apparently lost. Below is the text of his second journal, recording the June water detachment.

Excerpts from the
Journal of Occurrences on the route of
a party of Cherokee emigrants by Lt. E. Deas

6th June 1838—The present party of Cherokees consists mostly of Indians that were collected by the Troops and inhabited that portion of the Cherokee Country embraced within the limits of the State of Georgia, and were assembled at Ross' Landing E. Tenn. preparatory to setting out upon the Journey.

The number of the Party is about six hundred, but is not yet accurately known, as it was thought not expedient to attempt to make out the muster-rolls before starting. The Indians were brought into the Boats under guard & being necessarily somewhat crowded, any unnecessary delay whilst in that situation was by all means to be avoided on account of the health of the people. It was therefore thought best to set out from the point of assembly without waiting to muster the Party, leaving it to be done by the conductor after starting, when more accurate Rolls could probably be made than before setting out.

The route selected by the Superintendent is by water, and the Party was turned over to me to-day at Ross' landing, after having been placed on board of the Boats provided for it's Transportation to Decatur Ala. These consist of a small S. Boat [steamboat] of about 100 tons burthen, and 6 Flat-Boats, one with double cabins, (one over the other) of a large size. The others are middle sized Boats, but sufficiently capacious to transport the Party without being too much crowded.

The Boats having been lashed side by side, 3 on each side of the Steam Boat, all were got under way about noon and proceeded at about 4 or 5 miles an hour until we arrived near the Suck when it was necessary to separate them in passing thro' the mountains. The Suck, Boiling Pot, the Skillet, and the Frying Pan are names given to the different rapids found in the Tennessee River as it passes through the Cumberland Mountains.

The river here follows a very circuitous course a distance of 30 miles by water being only equal to 8 [miles] by land.

The Suck is the first and most difficult and dangerous of the rapids. The river here becomes very narrow and swift and the Banks on either side are rocky and steep, it being the point at which the stream passed thro' a gorge in the mountains. The S. Boat with one Flat on each side passed thro' with most of the people on board, but after getting thro' the most rapid water, it was found impossible to keep her in the channel, & in consequence was thrown upon the north Bank with some violence but luckily none of the people were injured although one of the Flats was a good deal mashed.

The other 4 boats came thro' two by two and the Party was encamped before dark as it was too late in the day to reach the fron[t] of the rapids in daylight.

The present party is accompanied by a guard of 23 men in order to prevent any desertions that might be attempted before leaving the limits of the Cherokee country.

7th June—The S. Boat and Flat Boats were got under weigh this morning and came thro' the remainder of the rapids separately. The first started at 8 o'clock, and all were got thro' by noon.

The Boats having been lashed side by side they continued to proceed at the rate of from 4 to 5 miles an hour thro' the remainder of the day.

8th June—Last night being clear and the moon nearly at the full the Boats continued to run until near daylight this morning when they were obliged to stop and separate owing to the Fog which suddenly sprung up. We passed Gunter's Landing about 9 o'clock and then continued to run (stopping once to wood) [to load wood for the engine] until dark, when the Boats were landed for the night 6 miles above decatur and such of the people as choose have gone ashore to sleep and cook. The weather has been remarkably fine since starting and the people generally healthy though there are several cases of sickness amongst the children.

9th June—The boats started this morning early and reached Decatur about 6 o'clock, but on arriving it was found that the R[ail] Road cars were not in readiness although they had been notified that the Party was approaching.

We have therefore been obliged to remain here to-day.

Two Locomotives have arrived in readiness to Transport the Party to Tuscumbia tomorrow.

10th June—This morning early the Indians and their Baggage were transferred from the Boats to the Rail Road cars.

About 32 cars were necessary to transport the Party, and no more could be employed for want of power in the Locomotive Engines.

The Indians therefore being necessarily crowded I determined not to take the Guard any further, as I heard the Steam Boat *Smelter* was waiting their arrival at the other end of the Rail Road, and in that case there would be no necessity for the Guard, as the Party would embark without any delay at Tuscumbia. On the arrival of the 1st train of cars at Tuscumbia Landing about 3 o'clock P.M. the Steam Boat was in readiness and took nearly half the Party on board but immediately set out for Waterloo at the foot of the Rapids without awaiting there for the 2nd Train of cars with the remainder of the party. In consequence when the 2nd Train arrived between 4 & 5 o'clock there being no Boat to receive the remainder of the Party on board they were necessarily encamped near the S. Boat Landing for the night, with the Guard having been sent back for the reasons above stated, and having no doubt that the Steam Boat *Smelter* would remain, drunkenness and disorder may be expected tonight. Nothing could be more unfortunate than the departure of the Boat at the moment the Party was on the point of reaching her.

11th June—As might be expected there was much drunkenness in camp last night and over one hundred of the Indians deserted. The remainder were conveyed from Tuscumbia Landing to Waterloo (30 miles) in one of the double deck keels and a Small Steam Boat.

The party was there established on board the *Smelter* and the two keels such as are described in the contract for Transportation and about 2 o'clock these Boats were got under weigh and have since continued to run from 10 to 12 miles an hour.

As there is room enough on board to accommodate the Party with sleeping room and the need thus being fine we shall continue to run thro' the night.

Until we reached Waterloo the Rations consisted of Flour, Corn-meal, & Bacon. At Tuscumbia yesterday I had purchased 4 days supply of Fresh Beef, but owing to the heat of the weather and the superstition of the Party most of it became spoiled and unfit for use before it could be issued when the Party was reassembled in the *Smelter* to-day.

12th June—The Boats continued to run until this forenoon at 11 o'clock (when a stop was made for wood) and reached Paducah between 4 and 5 P.M. I have Enrolled the Party as accurately & carefully as possible since leaving Tuscumbia and find the number to be 489.

Finding that the S. Boat and one Keel are sufficient to Transport the Party the other was left at Paducah this afternoon, and the rate of traveling is thereby much increased. We left Paducah about sunset and shall continue to run thro' the night.

The weather since starting with the present Party has been warm and as yet there has been no rain. The People have been generally healthy and there are but few cases of sickness at present and none of a dangerous character.

13th June—The Boats reached the mouth of the Ohio about midnight and have since continued to run stopping twice to wood in daylight. We passed Memphis this evening between 9 & 10 o'clock, but did not land. A small Boat was sent ashore to carry letters, and procure provisions.

The weather continues warm but the night being clear and calm the Boats will continue to run. The people remain generally healthy.

14th June—The Boats continued to run last night and to-day without interruption (except to wood in the forenoon) and reached Montgomery's Point at the Mouth of the White River at one o'clock P.M.

A Pilot for the Arkansas R. was then taken on board without landing, and we then entered White River passed thro' the cut-off into the Arkansas and continued to run until about sun-set, having ascended the Arkansas about 70 miles. Most of the people have gone on shore and Encamped for the night. The weather continues fine tho' warm and the Party remains generally healthy. A small quantity of F[resh] beef was procured last night at Memphis and was issued today.

The Arkansas River is low at present a circumstance very unusual at this particular season of the year.

15th June—The Boats got under way this morning at Sunrize and continued to run through the day stopping once to wood in the forenoon. We stopped for the night at a Wood Landing at dark, having run to-day about 70 miles, and many of the people have gone on shore and encamped for the night.

The weather continues warm and there has been a slight rain thro' the day. The Arkansas continues very nearly at a stand.

16th June—It rained very hard last night for a short time. The boats got under weigh this morning at day light and this afternoon about Sun-set landed 14 miles below Ft. Brooks.

The distance travelled to-day is about the same as yesterday not far from 70 miles.

A very perceptible rise has taken place in the River to-day and from the appearance of the water, it is probably caused by the melting of snows. The weather continues warm.

17th June—We started this morning after sun-rise and reached Lt. [Little] Rock about 8 A.M. The S. Boat was anchored in the stream a short time to prevent access to whiskey.

The river continuing to rise and as we have to lie by generally at night, I determined to leave the keel boat and give the people the main cabin of the S. Boat instead.

Thereby we shall travel much faster, and there is at the same time room enough for them by this arrangement.

We left Little Rock about 10 A.M. and continued to run until near Sun-Set, when we stopped for the night a few miles below Lewisburgh, and most of the people are now encamped on the shore. The weather continues fine and the party healthy. The River continued to rise yesterday and to-day and this evening it appears to be at a stand.

18th June—We set out this morning at daylight and continued to run with little interruption until dark, then stopped on the north bank opposite McLeans Bottom 2 miles above Titworth's Place.

The people have gone ashore to sleep and prepare food. They still remain generally healthy.

The weather to-day was very warm. The river has fallen about a foot here, within the last 24 hours.

19th June—The People were got on board and the Boats started this morning between 2 & 3 o'clock, but had to stop again before daylight—on account of heavy rain. They were got under weigh again at light and continued to run until 10 A.M. when we were again obliged to land on account of a slight accident to the Wheel. After 2 hours delay we again proceeded and reached Van Buren about 2 P.M. and stopped about ½ an hour in the Stream without landing the S. Boats.

We passed Ft. Smith between 3 and 4 P.M. and reached Fort Coffee a little before sun-set.

The Boats were landed opposite the Fort to procure food, and the people went on shore for the night as usual.

The weather continues extremely warm but the Party remains generally healthy.

Fort Coffee, 20 June—After the Party landed last evening I found that they had taken all of their Baggage out of the Boats and were desirous of stopping in this neighborhood.

The[y] evinced much pleasure at reaching their country in safety, and meeting some of their friends and acquaintances here, and finding that others of them are living not far off, they prefer remaining here to proceeding to Fort Gibson.

I should have preferred to deliver them at the latter place as there is water enough for the Boat to go up, at present, but at the same time considered it proper to consult their wishes.

After counselling together and with their friends from the vicinity they decided in favor of proceeding no further.

I therefore to-day discharged and paid-off the Agents & Physicians that accompanied the Party, who returned on the S. Boat *Smelter*.

This morning early an Express was dispatched by the Commanding officer with a letter from myself to the officer at Fort Gibson appointed to receive the Cherokees, giving information that the Party is at this place, awaiting to be mustered and to receive their subsistence.

Fort Coffee, 23rd June—Since arriving at this place I have issued a sufficient quantity of cotton domestic to the Indians for Tents to protect them from the weather. I have done so in consideration of their destitute condition, as they were for the most part separated from their homes in Georgia, without having the means or time to prepare for camping and it was also the opinions of the Physicians of the Party that the health of these people would suffer if not provided with some protection from the weather.

Last evening an Agent of Capt. J. R. Stephenson the Disbursing agent to receive the Cherokees arrived at this place and to-day I had the Party mustered in his presence. The number was found to be 489, as shewn by the Muster-Roll, no deaths having occurred upon the journey and no alteration having taken place since the Party was enrolled.

The foregoing Remarks embrace all matters of interest affecting the Indians, that came under my observation from the day of setting out upon the journey until the Party was to-day turned over to the Agent appointed to muster & Receive it.[8]

FEELINGS
OF DISCONTENT
June–September 1838

AFTER THE FIRST three detachments departed Ross's Landing in June 1838, General Nathaniel Smith, the superintendent of removal, left the landing to overtake each detachment to try to persuade the emigrants to accept blankets, clothing, and shelter. They had refused clothing and blankets earlier, for fear it might be construed as an acknowledgment of the Treaty of New Echota. They still hoped that John Ross would somehow manage to bring them back to their homes under a new arrangement.[1]

It was mid-June when the Cherokees and General Scott called a halt to emigrations for the remainder of the summer, the last two detachments having just left Ross's Landing two days apart.

One of those detachments, numbering 876 souls, was forcibly removed by the army under the command of Lieutenant R. H. K Whitely. The detachment traveled by water and rail to the Lewisburg sand bar, located near what is now Morrilton, Arkansas. From there, it was forced to go by land to the Cherokee Nation, as the water was too low for boat travel. Seventy-three deaths were reported in this group by the end of the 1,554-mile journey. The Whitely party also experienced a large number of desertions. Altogether, over 208 Indians deserted along the way.[2]

The detachment led by Captain G. S. Drane left on June 17. It included approximately 1,070 souls on departure. The Indians traveled by wagon, train, and foot from Ross's Landing across Moccasin Bend to Brown's Ferry, then on to Waterloo, Alabama. From Waterloo, they went by water to Little Rock. They then traveled overland by wagon to the Cherokee Nation West. Drane did not actually join the detachment until it reached Bellefonte, Alabama. The next morning, approximately half the detachment tried to desert. Thirty Alabama Volunteers, including a bugler, were hurriedly mustered into service to help round up the escapees. All but 225 were captured. Many deaths were reported along the way.[3]

The first item below is a report of the progress of the Whitely and Drane detachments by General Nathaniel Smith, the officer in charge of Cherokee emigration. His report disagrees with Whitely's journal, which states that his detachment left Little Rock on the steamboat *Tecumseh*. Drane did not leave behind a journal, but his official report is given following Smith's report.

General Nathaniel Smith's report to Major General Winfield Scott on the Whitely and Drane water detachments

Cherokee Agency East,
Augt 7th 1838

Maj'r Genl Winfield Scott,
Comdg Army Ch. Nation,
Sir:

Having just returned from accompanying two parties of Cherokee Emigrants, I have the honor to state that I left the *First*, conducted by Lt. Whitely, which started from Ross' Landing on the 12th June, at Little Rock on the 6th July, of that 728 arrived there in good health, 11 having died on the way. This party left Little Rock next day in the *Liverpool*, a small steamboat, with one large Keel in tow, for Fort Coffee or Fort Gibson. I returned & met Capt. Drane's party of about 800 at Waterloo, Ala. which was thirty days travelling but little over 200 miles by land.

Twenty two deaths had occurred, a great many of them were sick. I had them put on board a large Keel & Steam-boat, & left Waterloo on the evening of the 14th July. I accompanied them to Reynoldsburg, Tennessee, & left them, all extremely well pleased with their mode of travelling, on the 15th July. I was detained a few days in West Tennessee by indisposition. On my return home, at Winchester, Tenn., I saw a gentleman directly from Little Rock, who informed me that he saw the party land at that place on the 22nd July & that he was told five only had died on the boats.

Very respectfully,
Yr. Mo. Obt. Servt.
Nat Smith
Supt Cher. Em.[4]

Report of Captain G. S. Drane
to Major General Winfield Scott

Cherokee Agency, Tennessee
17th October 1838

General:

I have the honor to report that I was detailed for duty in the Indian Department as Disbursing agent on the 10th June 1838 & ordered to report myself for duty to Genl. N. Smith, principal Superintendant Cherokee Emigration on or before the 18th June 1838. I received orders to join & accompany a party of Cherokee Emigrants, about to leave Ross' Landing on the 17th June, not having received the necessary funds. I was not able to join the party until it reached Bellefonte, Alabama on the 25th June, on the morning of the 26th June when about to commence my march with the party, a Cherokee Indian arrived in camp from the Agency with a letter to one of the surgeons accompanying the party. He informed the emigrants that he had brought orders for them to return back to Ross' Landing. A large majority of them positively refused to proceed any further & unloaded the wagons & left the camp, every exertion was used on the part of the agents to bring them back, but with little success. A small company of mounted Volunteers soon assembled, with their assistance a large number was brought back—yet 225 escaped—the feelings of discontent among the Emigrants were so great that Genl N. Smith thought it advisable to accept the services of the volunteers as a guard to accompany the Indians to Waterloo, Alabama, & ordered me to muster them into the service of the United States for one month, unless sooner discharged. I am of the opinion this guard was of great service in preventing desertions & keeping the Indians from spreading through the country committing depredations, on my arrival at Waterloo, Alabama, I was ordered to muster the company out of the service, to discharge my teams & embark on board the steamboat *Smelter* & proceed to Fort Gibson by the way of the Arkansas river, I believed that route unhealthy, & requested Genl Smith to allow me to take the route by Boonsville, Missouri, the route selected previous to the party's leaving Ross' Landing. I was again positively ordered to proceed by the way of the Arkansas river, on the 14th July 1838 I embarked on board the steamer *Smelter* in obedience to his orders. [N]othing of importance occurred until the 22d July when the Steamer *Smelter* grounded 30 miles below Little Rock, she could proceed no further owing to the low stage of the water, here I was obliged to land the party on the bank of the river, the steamer *Smelter* left me early next morning, the same day I sent an express to Capt. Collins at Little Rock, Arkansas, for means of transportation, on the 25th July the steamer *Tecumse[h]* arrived & took the party on board, owing to low water, all the Indians able to walk was obliged to land at the sandbars & walk. I however reached Little Rock, Arkansas, on the 26th July— here I perceived I could proceed no further by water, I immediately made arrangements to procure wagons to proceed by land, with great difficulty I had collected near wagons sufficient but owing to the arrival of the steamer *Itaska* from Fort Coffee, & a slight rise in the river on the 2d of August the Indians refused to go by land, I had no means to compel them, I was compelled to discharge the wagons & charter the steamer *Itaska*, on the 4th August, I embarked the party & proceeded by water on *my* route, with great difficulty the steamboat reached Lewisburg bar 6 miles below the town on the 13th August, I immediately sent agents to collect wagons to proceed by land, with great labor & fatigue, I landed the party on the north bank of the river one mile below the town on the 17th August & on the 18th commenced my march up the north side of the river in hopes to find water more plenty, on the 4th September 1838 I arrived at Mrs. Webber's plantation in the Cherokee Nation west—with the party amounting to 635—which were mustered & received on the 7th September 1838—

The strength of the detachment leaving Ross' Landing, Tennessee, on the 17th June 1838—1072
Number of births while of the march—2
Total number—1074

Desertions while on the march between Ross' Landing, Tennessee, and Waterloo, Alabama—293
Number of deaths between Ross' Landing, Tennessee, & Waterloo Alabama & also from Waterloo to the Cherokee Nation West— 146
Number received & mustered in the Nation—635
[Total]—1074

I am now busily employed in arranging & settling my accounts to enable me to Furnish you with a statement of the average cost of each individual of the party. I am, sir, very respectfully

Yr obt servt
G. S. Drane
Capt. U.S.A.
Conductor & Disbursing Agent[5]

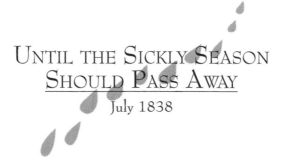

Until the Sickly Season Should Pass Away
July 1838

In a letter dated June 18, 1838, from Chattanooga, Colonel William Lindsay wrote Colonel W. J. Worth, "On this day there are 3000 Indians in my camp. I have been precluded from availing myself of the buildings at Ft. Poinsett from the fact that the measles are pervasive [at] that camp. At least 2000 Cherokees are destitute of shelter and within 3 miles of the measles. I have little doubt that three days more will bring 3000 more."[1]

Less than a month after the forced removal began, illness and death were attacking the camps and emigrant parties in epidemic proportions. Cherokees who had escaped from the Whitely and Drane detachments made their way back to the East and told of the sickness, deaths, and unhealthy food they had witnessed or experienced. A rumor also spread among the Cherokees that there had been a horrible steamboat accident resulting in several hundred fatalities among the emigrants.

While there were some mechanical problems and accidents on the steamboats and keelboats, no accident had caused death. The rumor may have originated with a terrible steamboat accident seven months earlier involving the Creek emigration. The steamboat *Monmouth*, carrying 611 Creeks, was cut in two by another steamboat, drowning over 300 emigrating Creek men, women, and children.[2]

On June 19, General Winfield Scott ordered the forced emigrations to be suspended until September 1 because of the heat and sickness of the season. Scott's action may also have been motivated by the complaints he was receiving from different quarters on how cruelly the emigration was being handled. His objective of a fast and efficient, yet compassionate, military operation had proven impossible. It was severely handicapped by the weather and the obstinacy of the Cherokees, who were putting up passive resistance by deserting and by refusing to accept supplies and to properly muster.[3]

On July 23, the members of the Cherokee Council sent a letter to General Scott formally asking permission to be allowed to remove themselves. Scott agreed to the proposal on the condition their emigration start by September 1. A few days later, the Cherokees held a council meeting at the Aquohee camp, south of the Hiwassee River near Charleston, Tennessee. At that meeting, they formally elected John Ross and six others as their official committee to oversee arrangements for self-removal.[4]

The contract Ross negotiated with the government set a cost of $65.88 per person for the entire journey. It allowed $.16 a day per person for rations and $.40 a day per horse or ox. Ross included costs for wagons, horses, drivers, physicians, interpreters, conductors, and other support personnel. On August 2, Ross and the Emigration Management Committee—Elijah Hicks, James Brown, Richard Taylor, Whitepath, Situwakee, and Edward Gunter—requested that soap be added to the list of emigration costs covered by the government. Scott agreed, although the army considered soap, coffee, and sugar to be unnecessary. Later, Ross transferred the contract to his brother Lewis, who was considered a better businessman.[5]

John Adair Bell, one of the Treaty Party leaders who had not yet emigrated, was furious when he learned of the arrangements the government had made with Ross. The Treaty Party feared that the funds being appropriated to Ross would deplete the money that would be made available for distribution. It also felt that the per capita removal allowance was lavish—forty dollars per person was more reasonable. It protested to Scott, who replied that the pro-treaty faction would be treated equally. Bell and the Treaty Party resented the power bestowed on Ross by the government in allowing him to control removal. They correctly feared that the power would carry over upon arrival in the West. General Scott and officials in Washington became suspicious of Bell and blamed him for stirring up problems in the Ross contingents. Scott ordered Lieutenant Deas to accompany the Treaty Party to the West, while the Ross-managed detachments went unaccompanied by military officers.[6]

Below are Ross's July 23, 1838, request to take charge of the emigration, Scott's reply to that request, and the Cherokee resolution adopted on July 26, 1838, authorizing Ross in his new role.

Letter from Chief John Ross and members of the Cherokee Council to Major General Winfield Scott

Aquohee Camp
July 23, 1838

Sir:

In respectfully presenting for your consideration the following suggestions in relation to the removal of the Cherokee people to the West, it may be proper very briefly to advert to certain facts which have an important bearing on the subject.

It is known to you, Sir, that the undersigned, Delegates of the Cherokee Nation, submitted to the Hon. the Secry. of War the project of a Treaty, on the basis of a removal of the Cherokee Nation from "all the Lands now occupied by them Eastward of the Mississippi" and on terms the most of which the Hon. Secry. expresses himself "not unwilling to grant." The present condition of the Cherokee people is such that all dispute as to the time of emigration is set at rest. Being already severed from their homes & their property: their persons being under the absolute control of the Commanding General. And being altogether dependent on the benevolence & humanity of that high officer for the suspension of their transportation to the West at a season and under circumstances in which sickness & death were to be apprehended to an alarming extent, all inducements to prolong their stay in this country are taken away. And however strong their attachment to the homes of their fathers may be: their interests and their wishes now, are to depart as early as may be consistent with their safety. Which will appear from the following extract from their proceedings on the subject.

"Resolved by the National Committee, & Council & People of the Cherokee Nation in General Council assembled, that it is the decided sense & desire, of this General Council, that the whole business of the emigration of our people, shall be undertaken by the Nation: and the Delegation are hereby advised to negotiate the necessary arrangements with the Commanding General for that purpose."

In conformity therefore with the wishes of our people and with the fact that the Delegation has been referred by the Hon. the Secry. of War to conclude the negotiation in relation to Emigration, with the Commanding General, in the Cherokee country.

We beg leave therefore very respectfully to propose: that the Cherokee Nation will undertake the whole business of removing their people to the West of the river Mississippi.

That, the Emigration shall commence, at the time stipulated in a pledge given, to you, by our people as a condition of the suspension of their Transportation, until the sickly season should pass away: unless prevented by some cause which shall appear reasonable to yourself.

That the per capita expense of removal be based on the calculation of one wagon & team & six riding horses being required for fifteen persons.

That the Cherokees shall have the selection of Physicians & such other persons as may be required for the safe & comfortable conducting of the several detachments to the place of destination; their compensation to be paid by the United States. We have the Honor to be, yr. obt. Hble. Servts.

Jno Ross
Elijah Hicks
James Brown
Edward Gunter
Saml Gunter [signed with his mark]
Situwakee [signed with his mark]
White Path
R. Taylor[7]

General Winfield Scott's reply

Head Quarters Eastern Division Cherokee Agency
July 25, 1838

Messrs. John Ross, E. Hicks, J. Brown, E. Gunter, S. Gunter, Sitewakee, White Path, & R. Taylor &c &c
Gentlemen

I have received your letter, submitting certain proposals, dated the 23rd instant.

On the part of the U. States, I am ready to place the whole business of completing the emigration of the Cherokee people, remaining east of the Mississippi (with an exception to be mentioned) to their new homes West of that river, in the hands of such functionaries of the Eastern Cherokees, as may exhibit to me from the same, due authority to undertake and carry thro' the emigration—on the following conditions: —

1. That the said functionaries & their people shall continue to observe & execute in good faith, the promises given to me in writing by certain Chiefs & head men for themselves & people, present & absent on the 19th ultimo.

2. That the said functionaries shall send intelligent Indian runners, to be furnished with written permissions signed by the Commanding General, in search of, & to cause to be brought in for the emigration, all Indian families & individuals who may remain out, & who are not Citizens of the U. States, or who have not received permission to remain in the States for the purpose of becoming denizens of the same.

3. That with the exception of such Indians as are, or who may have obtained permission to remain, in order to become, Citizens or denizens of the U. States, or of the States; also with the exception of such Indian families & individuals as may be permitted by the Commanding General to emigrate themselves *, the said Cherokee functionaries shall cause all their people, now remaining east, & who may at the time be able to travel, including fugitive Creeks among them, to be put in motion, in convenient detachments, either by land or water, & transported without unnecessary delays on the routes, to the Cherokee Country West of the Mississippi—beginning the movement as early as the first of September next, & continuing to send off parties at intervals, not exceeding three days, so that all the emigrants, able to

travel within the time, shall be in motion for the West by the _____ of the ensuing month (October).

Such Indians as, within that time, may not be able to travel by land, shall, if the rivers be not up, be permitted to remain until the next rise of waters, & in the mean time have, as attendants, a small number of their families or friends.

The foregoing Conditions being agreed to, the U. States, thro' me, are willing to stipulate to pay over to the Cherokee functionaries, from time to time, such portions of the moneys appropriated for the emigration as may seem reasonable to prepare for & carry it out.

I remain, gentlemen, &c
Winfield Scott

* Note for the Secretary of War

This exception is intended for the benefit of such of the Treaty making party as may not choose to remove under the directions of Mr. Ross & his associates.

Winfield Scott[8]

Resolution adopted by the Cherokee Nation conferring power on John Ross and others to undertake the emigration to the West

Resolved by the committee & council & people in General council convened,

That Messrs John Ross, Richd Taylor, Samuel Gunter, Edward Gunter, James Brown, Elijah Hicks, Situwakee & White Path, be, & they are hereby authorized & fully empowered on the part of the Cherokee Nation, to make & enter into any & all such arrangements with Mjr. Genl Winfield Scott on the part of the United States, which they may deem necessary & proper for effecting the entire removal of the Cherokee People from the East to the West side of the Mississippi river. And also to enter into such further arrangements with the commanding General in relation to the payment of such sums of money by the United States as may be needed for the removal & subsistence of all the Cherokee people.

And they are hereby further authorized, & empowered to make any such selection of persons as they may deem necessary to aid & assist in the said removal of the Cherokees to the western country.

Richd Taylor Prest N. Committee
Aquohee Camps, July 26th 1838

James D. Wofford, John F. Baldridge, Samuel Gunter, George Hicks, Thomas Foreman, Old Fields, Hair Conrad, George Still, James Hawkins, Na-hoo-lah, Chu-nas-la-has-ke, Elijah Hicks, William Proctor, Ka-loo-sa-te-he
Stephen Foreman, Clerk N. Committee
Going Snake, Speaker of the N. Council
James Spears, John Watts, Small Back, Wa-hatch-chee, The Bark, Money Crier, Soft Shell Turtle, Bean Stick, John Otterlifter, John Keys, White Path, Charles, Chu-wa-lu-gee, John Wane, Sith iwa-gee, Peter, Sweet Water, Farquah, The Coon
Jesse Bushyhead Clerk N. Council
Wa-loo-kah, Koolache, Tuff, Oosa-na-le, Choo-la-ske, Lying Fish, Ned, Michael Bridgemaker, Oosqua-loo-ter, Ta-na-e, Too-now-ee, Oo-ya-la-ga-th, In behalf of the People.

Approved In behalf of the People.
John Ross, Principal Chief
George Lowrey, Asst Pl Chief
Lewis Ross, Exe Council
Edward Gunter, Exe Council[9]

FOR THE COMFORT AND
WELL-BEING OF THIS PEOPLE
Summer 1838

AFTER THE CESSATION of emigration in late June 1838, the Cherokees, their slaves, a few remaining Creeks, and several missionaries had begun to settle in for a long, hard summer when a record drought hit the Southeast. Most of the Cherokees were spread out in camps in Tennessee around Red Clay, Ross's Landing, Cleveland, and Fort Cass in Charleston. There was another large camp in Will's Valley in Alabama.

The exact locations of many of these installations have not been ascertained, although a map of the Fort Cass area appears to fairly accurately place camps all over what is now the town of Charleston and the surrounding area. The camp at Rattle Snake Springs—one of several under the control of Fort Cass— is well documented.[1]

In Chattanooga, soldiers who were stationed at Ross's Landing during the removal later indicated that the military camps were moved several times between 1836 and the fall of 1838. The Cherokee camps may have been moved also as camp populations changed or as water sources became polluted. Reports indicate that the largest camps in the Chattanooga area were the Citico camps, which may have been located at the Tennessee River upstream of Ross's Landing near the railroad yards or near the mouth of South Chickamauga Creek. Other camps were identified as being near the head of Citico Creek at Indian Springs, which places them in front of what is now Memorial Hospital.[2]

In a report to General Winfield Scott on June 21, 1838, Colonel William Lindsay noted that 850 Cherokees were camped at Red Clay, 400 at Cleveland, 3,500 near the Cherokee Agency, and 2,500 in the vicinity of Ross's Landing. Stephen Hempstead, enrolling and issuing agent for the camps at the Cherokee Agency at Charleston, Tennessee, and the camps near Cleveland, reported on July 1, 1838, that he was issuing 7,217 rations daily. That number did not include a party from North Carolina that had arrived the previous day and had not yet made application for rations.[3]

In a letter to General Nathaniel Smith dated August 19, 1838, Dr. John S. Young reported that Colonel Lindsay had granted four hundred persons permission to leave the camps at Ross's Landing and "hunt for situations to suit themselves—some of the number remained at the homes they had previously occupied." That June, three families had been allowed to return to their homes at the foot of Lookout Mountain, eight or ten miles away.[4]

In another letter dated August 19 from Missionary Hill near Ross's Landing, an unknown officer reported to Captain Robert Anderson of the army's emigration department that he, Dr. John Young, and the Indian agents had tried to divide the Indians in the camps at Ross's Landing into parties for the purpose of emigration. However, the Cherokees wanted to emigrate under chiefs located at the Cherokee Agency.[5]

It's clear from the records and correspondence that after the initial cruelty of the collection, and after the first three detachments were driven at bayonet point on to the boats and ferry at Ross's Landing, several of the officers below General Scott became concerned about the health and comfort of the Cherokees. Large stations were set up to feed the masses, and physicians were hired for the camps. Vaccinations were ordered, camp boundaries were expanded to provide more privacy, and limited movement between camps was allowed so families could look for each other and prepare to remove as family units.

In mid-July, Captain John Page, the acting superintendent of Cherokee emigration while General Nathaniel Smith accompanied some of the water detachments west, wrote to the commissioner of Indian Affairs about the status of the camps and preparations for self-removal. He enclosed Dr. J. W. Lide's report about the number of physicians in the encampments and explained why they were necessary. He also explained that the final terms for self-removal had not been decided upon or communicated to him. Those documents are presented below, as is Dr. Lide's letter to Captain Page detailing the difficulties physicians encountered in serving the camps and discussing the illnesses suffered by the Cherokees.

Letter from Captain John Page to Commissioner of Indian Affairs C. A. Harris

Calhoun, Tennessee
25th July 1838

Sir

I have the honor to enclose herewith a list of the Physicians attending on the Cherokees. Situated as the camps are at this time I do not see how the number can be lessened. Camp

Ross is thirteen miles from this place, Ross' Landing about forty five miles and Fort Payne ninety five miles, each Physician is furnished with an Interpreter which cannot be dispensed with; There are seven issuing stands, and two issuing commisaries to each, and one Interpreter. There is no end to the bussiness that has to be done to keep up these different Depots. The wants and complaints of the Cherokees occupy all my time and Genl Smith being absent renders my situation verry unpleasant. If they go to Genl Scott, he sends them to me! I am making all preperations to commence the Emigration on the 1st of Sept. There is some probability of a party starting before that period.

Ross is in council endeavouring to do something towards moving themselves. I presume Genl Scott will determine how far he will acceed to Ross' proposition tomorrow or next day. I have requested him to decide as soon as possible, that I may know what to depend on [and] what the result may be[.] I will give you the earliest notice.

I have nothing of importance to communicate.

With Respect
I have the honor to be
Your Obt Servt

John Page, Capt & Acting Supt Cherokees[6]

Dr. J. W. Lide's list of physicians employed in the emigration and letter to Captain John Page

Name	Station	Cher. under charge
Dr. B. Cottle	Camp Ross	2000+
" Elizur Butler	" "	"
" A. M. Folger	East branch Mouse Creek (1st Encampt)	870+
" A. George	Fort Payne, Ala	900
" W. J. J. Morrow	Ross Landing	2000+

" J. M. Kennedy	Ross Landing	2000+
" J. Hunter	Agency Post	700
" J. H. Hertzel	Rattle Snake Springs	600
" ? H. Jordan	East branch Mouse Creek (2n Encampt)	1600
" J. W. Netherland	" " " "	" "
" Madison Cox	Bedwells' Springs	900
" A. W. Armstrong	Ches-too-ee	1300
" J. W. Edington	Ridge Encampt East of Agency	700
" ? J. Edwards	Upper "Cha-ta-te"	(number doubtful) say 600

Capt. John Page, USA
Prin. Disb. Agt. & Act. Supt. C.E.
Cher. Agency 20 July '38

Sir:

The above list of attending Physicians, their Stations, and the probable number of Cherokees under charge of each is made out conformably to your request of yesterday. [I]n reference to it, I have the honor to remark that in annexing the number at the different Encampments, entire precision and accuracy is not pretended. For I am not assured that the census had been taken with decided certainty and, even had it been, by frequent removals and change of place, the number is made to fluctuate with almost every day.

It is believed however, that the numbers set down are not very remote from the truth. I beg leave further to remark that when it is considered how scattered and dispersed are the family camps within the limits of each general encampment extending through the bounds of each Physicians care, miles of distance. The repugnance of many of the Indians (especially the mountain Cherokees) to the use of Medicine no matter how pressing the necessity. The delay and consumption of time at each camp of the sick occasioned by a lack of the Indian Language making all the communications between the sick and the Physician of necessity mediate instead of direct. It is at once apparent that any Practitioner could examine and treat daily, more than double the number of Patients, speaking his own Language, and any way habituated to the use of Medicine.

[I]n addition to these causes of delay, and the loss of time, the Physician finds it necessary in almost every instance with the view of securing the adoption of his Prescription to prepare and administer each dose of Medicine with his own hands. [A]nd here I take occasion to observe, that the Physicians employed, very generally, practic[e] a degree of perseverance and industry in their unremitting attention to the sick, and the prosecution of the business of "Vaccination," highly creditable to themselves, and advantageous, to the Service.

I wanto [sic] further remark that as a very natural result of collecting and marching to distant points of Rendezvous men, women and children of all ages and conditions, changing suddenly, and very materially all their habits of life, especially in reference to Regimin, Exercise, &c, with exposure to the intense heat that has prevailed in this country during the past and present months. We should feel little astonishment at finding a high grade of Diarrhea, hazardous Dysentery, and urgent Remittent Fever prevailing to a great and deplorably fatal extent. [I]n addition to this, Measles and Whooping Cough appeared epidemically among the Cherokees about the first of June which Diseases more generally much aggravated by the Circumstances connected with the assemblage. [A]ll these Diseases are now rife among them; and, it [must] seem from the facts that, not the least humane of the measures of Genl Scott devised for the comfort and well being of this People was his order about the first of June to increase the number of attending Physicians.

[T]he number was increased accordingly; and, under a press of circumstances, that continue to exist and likely by no means to abate during the present and succeeding months. The mortality, hitherto great, I am happy to inform you, is manifestly diminishing. A fact ascribable not so much to the decline of Disease as the growing reconciliation of the Indians to the use of Medicine and regulated Regimen.

I am Sir, Very Respectfully
Your Obt Servant

J. W. Lide, Dir Phys. C.E.[7]

THE SADNESS
OF THE HEART
August 1838

THE FIRST GROUP to leave the Cherokee Agency at Charleston under John Ross's management was the Hair Conrad detachment. It departed the camps on August 28, 1838, three days ahead of the scheduled date of September 1. According to Captain John Page's records, this detachment consisted of 710 people; according to John Ross's records, the number was 729. The group included approximately thirty-six wagons and teams. Captain J. R. Stephenson, the receiving agent at Fort Gibson, recorded 654 Cherokees arriving in the West with the first detachment. There were approximately nine births, fifty-four deaths, and twenty-four desertions.

The second detachment left the Cherokee Agency on September 1 and was conducted by Elijah Hicks. It departed with 858 or 859 people and arrived with approximately 744. Five births and thirty-four deaths were reported along the trail.[1]

The first two detachments traveled only eighteen or twenty miles to Blythe's Ferry at the Tennessee River. General Winfield Scott stopped them at the river because of reports that "water for persons and horses can not be found, & the dust & heat are such as to endanger the lives of all. The first and second parties will therefore halt for a while."[2]

Other detachments were held at the Cherokee Agency until reports of rain on the route of emigration brought confidence that water would be plentiful. In a letter to C. A. Harris, Captain Page reported that he suspected that the cessation of emigration was also a delaying tactic on the part of Ross.[3]

During the weeks that the detachments were camped at Blythe's Ferry waiting to resume their march, Hair Conrad became ill and was replaced by Daniel Colston as conductor of the first detachment.[4] Colston was later implicated in the deaths of the Ridges and Elias Boudinot in 1839.

When travel resumed, First Lieutenant H. L. Scott of the Fourth Infantry was sent out eighty miles along the route taken by the first two emigrating parties. He reported back to General Scott that

> the first party that crossed the Tennessee River at Blythe's Ferry consisted of 830 Cherokees conducted by Mr. E. Hicks, a native. The march of this party through the country was perfectly orderly, and at the time that I overtook them they were at McMinnville, five days march from Blythe's ferry. The second party was conducted by Mr. Colston, a native, and the march of his party through the country was characterized by the same orderly conduct that distinguished the party that preceded him, this party at the time that I passed them on my return, was two days march from McMinnville.
>
> The greatest harmony & cheerfulness prevails in these two detachments, & with the exception of four deaths among

the children, they have met with no mishaps, & encountered no difficulties thus far on the route.[5]

William Shorey Coodey, the author of the narrative below, was the nephew of John Ross. Coodey was sent to Washington as a delegate representing the Cherokee Nation in 1831 and 1832 to present grievances against the state of Georgia for intrusions on Cherokee lands.[6] He witnessed the departure of the first detachment on August 28 from the Cherokee Agency and recorded his memories in a poignant letter in 1840 to John Howard Payne, author of the ballad "Home Sweet Home." Payne was a friend of the Cherokees who planned to publish a history of the tribe. He advised John Ross on the publication of two pamphlets arguing against removal. While Payne was visiting Ross at his home at Red Hill in November 1835, both men were arrested by the Geogia Guard and hauled to Spring Place on trumped-up charges.[7]

Letter from Cherokee leader William Shorey Coodey to John Howard Payne on the departure of a land detachment

Washington City,
August 13, 1840

The entire Cherokee population were captured by the U.S. troops under General Scott in 1838 and marched, to principally, upon the border of Tennessee where they were encamped in large bodies until the time for their final removal west. At one of these encampments, twelve miles south of the Agency, and Head Quarters of Genl. Scott, was organised the first detachment for marching under the arrangement committing the whole management of the emigration into the hands of the Cherokees themselves.

The first of Septer. was fixed as the time for a part to be in motion on the route. Much anxiety was felt, and great exertions made by the Cherokees to comply with everything reasonably to be expected of them, and it was determined that the first detachment should move in the last days of August.

I left the Agency on the 27th, after night, and reached the encampment, above alluded to, early the following morning, for the purpose of aiding in the arrangements necessary to get a portion in motion on that day, the remainder to follow the next day and come up while the first were crossing the Tennessee River, about twenty five miles distant.

At noon all was in readiness for moving. The trains were stretched out in a line along the road through a heavy forest, groups of persons formed about each waggon, others shaking the hand of some sick friend or relative who would be left behind. The temporary camps covered with boards and some of bark, that for three summer months had been their only shelter and *home* were crackling and falling under a blazing flame. The day was bright and beautiful, but a gloomy thoughtfulness was strongly depicted in the lineaments of every face. In all the bustle of preparation there was a silence and stillness of the voice that betrayed the sadness of the heart.

At length the word was given to *move on*. I glanced along the line and the form of Going Snake, an aged and respected chief whose head eighty winters had whitened, mounted on his favorite poney passed before me and lead the way in advance, followed by a number of young men on horse back.

At this very moment a low sound of distant thunder fell on my ear. In almost an exact western direction a dark spiral cloud was rising above the horizon and sent forth a murmur I almost fancied a voice of divine indignation for the wrongs of my poor and unhappy countrymen, driven by *brutal* power from all they loved and cherished in the land of their fathers, to gratify the cravings of avarice. The sun was unclouded—no rain fell—the thunder rolled away and seemed hushed in the distance. The scene around and before me, and in the elements above, were peculiarly impressive & singular. It was at once spoken of by several persons near me, and looked upon as ominous of some future event in the West. In several letters written to my friends on the same evening I alluded to the circumstances, so strong was the effect on my own mind, at the time.[8]

A Year of
Spiritual Darkness
June and December 1838

When the Reverend Daniel Sabin Butrick arrived in Cherokee country, he was assigned to the mission at Spring Place, Georgia. He was later reassigned to the Carmel Mission—or Taloney, as the Cherokees preferred to call it. In the spring of 1836, the Reverend and Mrs. Butrick moved to the mission at Brainerd when the school at Carmel closed. Most of the Cherokee families had left Carmel due to oppressive Georgia laws and after forfeiting their lands in the land lottery.[1]

The Reverend Butrick was one of several missionaries who signed memorials in support of Cherokee rights. In 1831, when Georgia began arresting missionaries it considered to be troublemakers, Butrick was included.[2]

By the time of the 1838 removal, Butrick had lived and ministered in Cherokee territory for twenty years. He kept a journal recording many of the events that occurred, the people he met, and the traditions he observed. Butrick was an opponent of the Treaty of New Echota and the terrible events that transpired during the removal. He felt it was his duty to do what he could for the suffering Cherokees who passed by the Brainerd Mission on their way to camps or to Ross's Landing to be crowded on to boats. In his journal, he described many of the degradations suffered by the Cherokees, their slaves, and approximately five hundred Creeks who had taken refuge in Cherokee territory the previous year, trying to escape that tribe's tragic expulsion from the East.[3]

When Cherokee-managed emigrations began in the fall of 1838, Butrick cast his lot with the Richard Taylor detachment. They left Ross's Landing in September and stopped at Vann's Town, where they camped for some time before crossing the Tennessee River at Dallas on November 1. They followed approximately the same route as an earlier detachment led by James Brown and Lewis Hilderbrand that went through McMinnville, Tennessee, then followed essentially the same northern route as many of the other Ross detachments. Richard Taylor's detachment arrived at its destination on March 24, 1839. According to John Ross's count, the Taylor party had 1,029 souls. Captain Page's records indicated that 897 started the trip. Captain Stephenson's records showed that 942 finished the trip. The detachment reported fifty-five deaths and fifteen births. It was one of the higher death tolls, though at least two other detachments—Situwakee and Old Fields'—reported more deaths.[4]

Two excerpts from Butrick's journal are included below.

The first is from June 1838. The dates of the entries are confusing. They are presented here in the order they were written in the journal, though that is not necessarily the order in which the events occurred. At the time of the first two entries, the army and the militia were still moving the Cherokees, most of whom were from Georgia, to Ross's Landing in preparation for loading them on flatboats to be hauled down the Tennessee River. By June 17, the date of the third June entry in Butrick's journal, the last detachment had left Ross's Landing. That detachment of approximately 1,070 people (according to Captain Page's count) traveled by wagon train to Waterloo, Alabama, then by water. Butrick's entries for June describe the suffering in the temporary camps where the Cherokees waited for departure and the rough handling by the army as they were marched to the camps or loaded on to boats. At one point in his journal, Butrick comments that General Scott's humane orders were obeyed according to the disposition of individual officers and their men.[5]

The second excerpt describes life on the road for the Taylor detachment. It is December, and the detachment is in Illinois. It must stop due to snow. Butrick tells how the emigration has come to a virtual standstill due to ice on the Ohio and Mississippi Rivers. Still, he is fortunate in that many kind white people have provided him and his wife shelter along the road and that he has not had to sleep in a tent, under a wagon, or in the open every night, as have the suffering Cherokees. Butrick also expresses his resentment toward Elias Boudinot, the former editor of the *Cherokee Phoenix*. He and many Cherokees felt Boudinot betrayed the tribe when he signed the Treaty of New Echota and emigrated west in 1837.

Excerpts from the journal of the Reverend Daniel Sabine Butrick

EXCERPT 1

Monday [June 11 or 18, 1838]—Went to the camps. Saw many of the poor Creeks. Enquired for Soft Shell Turtle, but as his tent was some distance off, I did not visit him. He is a chief of some note, from Hightower.

When the soldiers were taking the people, he, with nearly thirty others, fled to a mountain. They were discovered a few days ago, and brought to the camps. He was handcuffed, and his hands considerably swollen when he came last week.

As Moses' father in law, Old Bear, wishes to live near Brainerd, we obtained permission for him to do so. The weather being extremely warm and dry, many of the Cherokees are sick, especially at Calhoon [Calhoun], where, we understand from four to ten die in a day.

On returning from the camps was overtaken by a gentleman who had been with a boat load of dear Cherokee prisoners. Of the second boat load, he says thirty had died when he met them at Waterloo, and great sickness was prevailing.

Just [last] night our dear sister Jane short arrow, and her daughter called and ate supper. Her child is sick. Her husband and most of her children were driven off to the West, while she was detained by the sickness of her eldest daughter. She is now in great trouble.

Sabbath June 10—By permission we attempted to hold a meeting at the camps. On the way we passed a company of nearly 1,000 poor Cherokee prisoners, under a formidable guard of soldiers. These arrived soon after us, and were ushered into the iron grasp of other soldiers. Among these was our aged br. January, the father of br. Epenetus. About noon we collected a few, and spent sometime in prayer. Not long however, after commencing, we were interrupted by the arrival of another company of prisoners, consisting of about 1,000.

As we were leaving the camps we passed a woman lying senseless. On her arrival today, being unwell, she was not able to endure the sight of some friends she saw in the camps, and immediately on seeing them, she fainted and fell to the ground.

When the company was driven from Lafayette [Georgia], one woman fainted and fell in the road, as she was driven on.

Another in the company, being seized with the pains of childbirth, stopped with her mother an hour or two, and then with her child, assisted by her aged mother went on to overtake her friends.

On returning to Brainerd, the reflections on the occurences of the day seemed overwhelming. Groaning was my only repast. It seemed a luxury to groan and weep. During this week I again visited the camps, and spoke to general Smith, the agent for removing the Indians respecting br. Epenetus, and urged that he might not be sent away while his son was at our house, and I thought he said he should not. He called Epenetus, & said, If you are called on to start, come to me, and say that your son is with Mr. Butrick. I felt satisfied then that he would not be sent away without our knowing it. His youngest child, a lovely little girl about 18 months old, was sick with the dysentery.

The Cherokees had been kept on a small spot, surrounded by a strong guard, under such circumstances that it would seem impossible for male or female to secrete themselves from the gaze of the multitudes for any purpose whatever, unless by hanging up some cloth in their tents, and there they had no vessel for private use. But now the limits were somewhat enlarged, yet it is evident that from their first arrest they were obliged to live very much like brute animals; and during their travels, were obliged at night to lie down on the naked ground, in the open air, exposed to wind and rain, and herd together, men women and children, like droves of hogs, and in this way, many are hastening to a premature grave. If all the infants under six months or a year and all the aged over sixty had been killed directly, and one fourth of the remainder, and the residue suffered to continue under favorable circumstances till they could move with safety, a vast amount of expense and suffering would apparently have been saved, and as many lives, or nearly as many, have been spared to witness the returns of another year as will now. Driving them under such circumstances, and then forcing them into filthy boats, to overflowing in this hot season, landing them at Little rock, a most sickly place, to wait other means of conveyance 200 miles up the Arkansas river, is only a most expensive and painful way of putting the poor people to death.

The first company sent down the river, including those dear trembling doves who spent a night at our house, were, it appears, literally crammed into the boat. There was, we understand, a flat bottom boat, 100 feet long, 20 feet wide, and two stories high, fastened to an old steam boat. This was so filled that the timbers began to crack and give way, and the boat itself was on the point of sinking. Some of the poor inmates were of course taken out, while this boat was lashed to the steam boat, and some other small boats were brought to take in those who had been recalled. Twelve hundred, it is said, were hurried off in this manner at one time.

Who would think of crowding men, women and children, sick and well, into a boat together, with little, if any more room or accommodations than would be allowed to swine taken to market? In that company were some of our dear brethren and sisters. But the insulting cry must be obeyed. "Fly like a timorous trembling dove. To distant woods and mountains fly."

The second company I had the painful pleasure to see marched down to the river. This consisted of about fifteen hundred. They were driven to the bank of the river, and there guarded all night, to lie down like so many animals on the naked ground. On returning from this melancholy scene, br. Vail and myself went to the camps, and though we could not pass the guard, yet we saw our dear br. Epenetus, and had the pleasure of bidding him good night, though we little thought, for that last time in his native land.

Sabbath June 17—Br. Wilookah brought us a message from br. Epenetus. He saw him on the bank of the river, as he and his family were about to be thrust into the boat. Epenetus told him to tell us he wanted to see us, and that he told general Smith he wanted to see his son living with us, but that general Smith told him he could afford him no relief, but he must go immediately. He wished us therefore to take care of his son, and fetch him with us, should we go to the West; and also to have br. Vail sell his horse or send him to the West. He had a horse when taken, on which his wife was riding, and on arriving at the camps, put it into the hands of br. Vail. He had at home a yoke of oxen, a number of cows, and other creatures. But these, together with all his house-hold furniture and bedding, are lost forever, doubtless, to him. Thus our dear Cherokees were stripped of all their little store, which they have been so happily laying up for a few years past. And at the same time the coffers of some of their rich oppressors have been crowded to overflowing.

The master of the steam boat who took our friends to Mussle [Muscle] shoals, had $4,000 for his reward. This trip he performed in eight days.

Being informed that some of our friends from Rolling Water had arrived, I endeavored, as soon as convenient to look them up, but found that our dear br. Isaac and his children, some of whom were small, had been hurried off down the river, while his wife and eldest daughter were back at Taloney. The family at first, were all taken together, and with others, driven to Taloney about thirty miles. There the eldest daughter, a young married woman was confined in childbed [childbirth], and left for the present with her mother & husband. But before they were able to travel so as to get to the camps, the father & all the children but an infant and the daughter above mentioned, were driven away, never perhaps again to welcome the delinquent members of their family.

On this day i.e. June 17, we were called to follow the remains of a poor Cherokee woman to the grave. A few days ago, some families obtained permission to camp near us, and among them were two persons brought on litters, nearly gone with the consumption. One of these was a woman of about middle age, and the other a young man. On Friday, we were told that the woman was apparently dying. Br. Vail and myself went to see her. She enquired if we thought her dying. I knelt down and prayed for her dear departing soul. I was at once overcome, and wept aloud in contemplating the condition of these dear sick people. She seemed prepared for her departure. She died on Saturday.

EXCERPT 2

Tuesday [December 18, 1838]—As we do not start today, it is thought best to move onto dryer ground. My own health failed, had a high fever in the afternoon, and took an emetic [vomit inducer]. After the operation of this, I was seized with a severe pain in my right side, which increased till sometime in the night, when the physician bled me, and put a poultice of mustard seed on my side, which afforded relief.

Wednesday [December 19]—We travelled about 6 miles, and camped. Had a comfortable night.

Thursday [December 20]—As several waggons and some sick persons are still behind, we wait today for them.

This morning a little child about 10 years old died.

Previous to starting on this journey, I determined to let it be a journey of prayer, and to devote much time every day to that sacred duty, but instead of this, I have very strangely neglected prayer. In the morning our time is employed in taking our bed etc. from the little waggon in which we sleep, to the large waggon which carries it, replacing the seat, getting water, cooking breakfast, putting up things, harnessing etc. Soon we are hurried on by the waggons we accompany to the next encampment. Here we have to und[o] what we did in the morning, put up our tent, get wood, and water, prepare supper, fix our bed etc. We often become much fatigued by the time we get our fire prepared.

I know that all this cannot justify a neglect of prayer. I think my own heart is more peculiarly depraved, especially as respects impatient & angry feelings. And further, I have no pleasing anticipations about arriving at the Arkansas. Mr. [Samuel] Worcester will doubtless wish to sustain, or at least, excuse Mr. [Elias] Boudinot in the course he has taken; and as the A. Board [American Board of Commissioners for Foreign Missions] have received Mr. Boudinot as an assistant missionary at the west, they doubtless look over his conduct in making the treaty, yet the mission churches in the nation do not, and by attempting to crowd him into their favour, without any acknowledgement on his part, we should only prove, or seem to prove to them, that we were interested with him, and plunge the mission of the A. Board like lead in the mighty waters.

Mr. Taylor said long ago, if I mistake not, that he could not commune with Mr. Boudinot. Br. Mills, an elder in Haweis church said the same, and would not attend the communion when Mrssrs. Chamberlain & Potter held it at Mr. J[ohn] Ridge's, because he was opposed to the measures they were taking. Maj. Lowrey, an elder in Willstown [Alabama] church had spoken decidedly against the measures adopted by the treaty party. Knowing the minds of the church, I felt that the case called for a thorough and candid investigation by some ecclesiastical body, and therefore I gave the brethren of Brainerd church an opportunity to express their feelings on the subject, hoping that this might bring the case before some council or presbytery, by which it might be examined and decided in a proper manner, though it is very doubtful whether I live to reach that place.

The little boy who died last night was buried today in a

coffin made of puncheons.

Friday [December 21]—We proceeded six miles to a very pleasant spot, to remain till Monday.

Saturday [December 22]—This morning two children died with the bowel complaint. Towards night the wind arose, and the air turning cold, I did not attend the prayer meeting.

Sabbath [December 23]—We have peculiar cause of gratitude for the preservation of the last night. The wind blew a gale nearly the whole night, and seemed to threaten almost certain calamity, both by scattering the fire through the leaves and tents, and also by throwing limbs, trees etc. upon our heads. But those eyes which never slumber watched over us, and preserved us in safety, though we had but little sleep.

The weather is now piercing cold, so that we despair of holding any public meeting. I consulted Mr. Taylor and we concluded to hold a prayer meeting in some tent, and accordingly met in the tent of br. J. Pridget.

Monday & Tuesday [December 24 and 25]—Travelled about 15 miles.

Tuesday about noon, the linch pin came out of one end of the fore axletree, the wheel came off and the end of the axletree, falling on the frozen ground broke, so that we had much trouble to get on to a waggon maker 6 miles forward. My dear wife had to walk considerably, & I became quite fatigued.

We now called for lodgings at the house where we were to get our work done. The house was rather open & contained but one room, yet the family at length consented to our stay. Here our bodies were refreshed, but our souls pained. The workman, the man of the house, came home a little before night in a high state on intoxication, & almost every word was accompanied with an oath. We hastened to bed, not considering it possible to have family worship. None of this family can read or write. The workman, i.e. the waggon maker is about 60 years old, and presents an awful spectacle. There are five adults in the family, yet none, to read. The woman says also that their preacher himself sometimes gets drunk. He is a Schismatic, or Bible Christian. He does not exclude any from the church, not even for drinking, because he says, all must grow together till the harvest.

Thus far the citizens of Illinois appear more & more pitiable. They seem not only low in all their manners, but ignorant, poor, and ill humoured. They have no slaves, but in general, as far as we have seen, they seem to be hankering after these leeks of Egypt, and because they cannot have slaves, let their work go undone. We see nothing like schools in the country.

Wednesday [December 26]—The morning is excessively cold. Rode to the encampment, one mile, and found our dear Cherokees comfortable in their tents. Saw Mr. Taylor, he says they will remain today where they are.

It is said the detachments now at the Mississippi are stopped by floating ice, and Mr. Hilderbrand's detachment is stopped by the same means at the Ohio R.

After breakfast my dear wife accompanied me to the camps, where we put down our tent, prepared wood for the night, but on returning for our carryall found it would be done to sleep in, and therefore we were obliged again to sleep at the house.

Thursday [December 27]—We proceeded with the detachment about 6 miles, where we camped for the week. Here the snow increased to three or four inches, and the weather was excessively cold.

Friday & Saturday [December 28 and 29]—Afflicted with a

fever afternoons & a cough during the night. So also on the Sabbath was unable to attend meeting. Our dear br. Wilooka had a meeting.

It is distressing to reflect on the situation of the nation. One detachment stopped at the Ohio River, two at the Mississippi, one four miles this side, one 16 miles this side, one 18 miles, and one 3 miles behind us. In all these detachments, comprising about 8,000 souls, there is now a vast amount of sickness, and many deaths. Six have died within a short time in Maj. [James] Brown's company, and in this detachment of Mr. Taylor's there are more or less affected with sickness in almost every tent; and yet all are houseless & homeless in a strange land, and in a cold region exposed to weather almost unknown in their native country. But they are prisoners. True, their own chiefs have directly hold of their hands, yet the U. States officers hold the chiefs with an iron grasp, so that they are obliged to lead the people according to their directions in executing effectually that Schermerhorn treaty.

Monday, Dec. 31—This morning we were permitted to read the texts for this last day of the year. O what a year it has been! O what a sweeping wind has gone over, and carried its thousands into the grave; while thousands of others have been tortured and scarcely survive, and the whole nation comparatively thrown out of house & home during this most dreary winter.

And why? As coming from God, we know it is just. But what have they done to the U. States? Have they violated any treaty? or any intercourse law; or abused any of the agents or officers of the U. States? Or have they refused to accomodate U. States citizens when passing through the country? No such thing is pretended. For what crime then was this whole nation doomed to this perpetual death? This almost unheard of suffering? Simply because they would not agree to a principle which would be at once death to their national existence, viz. that a few unauthorized individuals might at any time, set aside the authority of the national council & principal chief, and in opposition to the declared will of the nation, dispose of the whole public domain, as well as the private property of individuals, and render the whole nation houseless & homeless at pleasure. Such a treaty the President of the U. States sanctioned, the Senate ratified, and the military force was found ready to execute. And now we see some of the effects.

The year past has been a year of spiritual darkness. We have had but few happy seasons, and as for myself, I have by no means been faithful to my trust. I have wanted faith & love & zeal. A great part of the time my heart has been grieved to hear the awful profanements and see the scenes of wickedness which have been brought before us.[6]

HAIL, RAIN, WIND AND THUNDER
March 1839

DRS. W. J. J. MORROW and John M. Kennedy were assigned to the camps at Ross's Landing as attending physicians during the summer of 1838. Dr. Morrow's brother, George D. Morrow, served as attending physician on the Lieutenant R. H. K. Whitely water detachment, which left Ross's Landing in mid-June 1838 and arrived in Arkansas in August. Both Morrows accompanied the Richard Taylor detachment from Ross's Landing in September and followed the Old Harrison Pike north to Vann's Town (now Harrison), where they camped for some time before crossing the Tennessee River at Dallas. The Morrows traveled with the same detachment as the Reverend Daniel S. Butrick, whose journal is described in the previous chapter. Dr. Kennedy accompanied the John Drew detachment.[1]

Dr. W. J. J. Morrow kept a journal of his trip on the Trail of Tears. Only the portions of the journal dealing with the journey from Missouri to Fort Gibson and the trip back survive. The excerpt below begins shortly after the detachment crosses the Illinois River and describes the trip to the Cherokee Nation in the West. Several of the dates in the Morrow and Butrick journals disagree by approximately one week but describe some of the same events, including the pitiful incident of a child's head being run over by a wagon. The reason for the discrepancies is unclear. It's possible that either Butrick or Morrow was writing the events down after the fact and confused some dates or wrote some of the events slightly out of order.[2]

Dr. Morrow preferred to stay in private homes or taverns during the journey. His brother George served as his assistant and remained in the camps through most of the trip.[3] Morrow's journal contrasts sharply with Butrick's in the way he describes the journey. Clearly, Morrow remained detached from the emigrants in both physical and emotional terms. This emigrating party had one of the higher death tolls, fifty-five deaths being reported on the road.

Excerpts from the journal of Dr. W. J. J. Morrow

March 2nd— . . . Snow storm from the north. Mrs. Thompson came to camp. Her husband, Johnston Thompson, died at Potosi [Missouri]. The detachment moved one and a half miles below Bates' on Little Piney. . . . The coldest day we have traveled.

March 3rd— . . . It was very cold and the detachment did not move.

March 4th— . . . Traveled to Harrison's on Big Piney— very cold, —distance ten miles. . . . James Harrison, two miles below Bates's . . . [Harrison] a mean man . . . will not let any person connected with the organization [emigration party] stay with him.

March 5th—[The party traveled twelve miles to Waynesville, on Roberdcan Creek, a branch of the Gasconade.] Clear and pleasant day. Stayed at Col. Swink's, a genteel man and pretty wife, and quite familiar.

March 6th—The detachment made a late start—the morning warm, wind from the south, look out for rain. Traveled fourteen miles to the Gasconade River, at Starks's, through a barren and sterile country. The day continued pleasant. Sydney Roberts in this neighborhood.

March 7th— . . . Fine morning, —made an early start; reached our encampment at Beans', on the Osage, against ten o'clock—distance ten miles. Still a barren country, —Beans' a mean house.

March 8th— . . . Traveled to Grigsby's, ten miles. . . . Same kind of country. Grigsby's farm a fine one . . .

March 9th—Traveled eleven miles to a creek four miles southwest of Park's, seven miles from Grigsby's. Went on to Burnett's myself with Cox, six miles beyond the encampment. . . .

March 10th, Sunday, —The detachment came up to Burnett's early in the morning—fine, pleasant day. [The Reverend Daniel S.] Buttrick preached. Burnett farm a fine one. Col. Burnett has bought a preemption twenty miles southwest of Burnett's.

March 11th— . . . A fine day. . . Detachment off early— Traveled ten miles to Neavis'.

March 12th— . . . The detachment started before day. The weather turned cold during night and it was snowing in the morning.

March 13th—Cold morning; came on to Springfield, eight miles. Got no letter from home, much disappointed. Alfred Indian living here. Sprin[g]field is a rich country. Many Indians got drunk.

March 14th—Fine morning; clear and calm. General Smith, tavern keeper, a fine fellow. Traveled to Dyer's/Bell Tavern/12 miles.

March 15th—Clear and fine morning. Traveled seventeen miles to Allen's, through a desert. Got a mean dinner. Didn't like the place and went two and a half miles to Igou's. Parr, one half mile south of Allen's said to be a good place. A wagon ran over a little Indian's head; had to go to camp and see him. Staid [stayed] in camp the first time since I left Gore's, in Illinois.

March 16th—Traveled twelve miles to Lock's, in Barry County, on Flat Creek, a branch of White River. Lock a gambler and hunter. Did not sleep much. The girls and boys talked and laughed all night. A fine, pleasant day.

Sunday, March 17th—Traveled up Flat Creek fifteen miles to McMurtres'. Ate dinner at Mason's, two miles northeast of McMurtre's—fine day.

March 18th—Clear and warm, traveled through Washburn's Pararie [Prairie] and to Pratt's, eighteen miles. Crossed the line of Arkansas and Missouri, near Meek's and Sugar Creek, seven miles northeast of Pratt's. Midnight, hail, rain, wind and thunder.

Tuesday, March 19th— . . . Rain all day—did not travel.

Wednesday, March 20th— . . . Cloudy and cool. Traveled fifteen miles to the X Hollows. Ate dinner at Housely's, and came on five miles to Fitzgerald's, in company with Cox, Fields, Henegar, and George D. Morrow. A mean house.

Thursday March 21st—Cloudy and cool. Passed through Fayetteville [Arkansas] and met the detachment at Cunningham's, three miles from town. Did not get a letter at town. Much disappointed. Fayetteville in Washington County. Fertile land around it. Beautiful situation. A good courthouse, bank-house and some other good buildings. Got a mean dinner a[t] the brick tavern. From Cunningham's we traveled to Col. Thomason's, on the twenty-second of March, sixteen miles, and on Saturday, the twenty-third, we arrived at the Wood Alley, in the Cherokee Nation, west three miles from the boundary line.

March 24th— . . . Most of the Indians turned over to the government. Settled my business and on Monday left for John Ross's headquarters. Traveled down Barren Fork of Illinois and over to the main river and took lodgings at Key's. Jim Brown there.

March 26th—Left after breakfast. Saw C. N. Cowan; got six hundred dollars, arrived at Coody's for dinner, ten miles, got dinner and went down to Fort Gibson, ten miles. Returned from Fort Gibson to Mrs. Coody's and staid all night; saw Bety Cheek there.

March 27th—Came up to Coody's tried to get my business settled, —did not accomplish my object until Sunday, ten o'clock, when we, Brother George J. J. Fields and Black George started for home and traveled to Smith's, eighteen miles.[4]

ONE OLD MAN
NAMED TSALI
November–December 1838

THE TRAGIC STORY of Tsali (or Charley) and his family has become a symbol of the removal and the long struggle of the North Carolina Cherokees to retain their eastern homelands.

Tsali and his family, which included his wife, three sons, son-in-law, and assorted relatives, were captured by soldiers under the command of Lieutenant A. J. Smith. As they were being taken to Fort Cass for removal to the West, a scuffle ensued, and two soldiers were killed. Tsali and his family and other prisoners escaped into the mountains, where they hid for several weeks.[1]

In November, William Holland Thomas, the white leader of the Oconaluftee Cherokees, persuaded a group of Cherokees led by Euchella, also known as U'tsălă or Lichen, to hunt for Tsali's hiding place. Euchella's Cherokees helped capture and execute four of the fugitives. Tsali's son-in-law and sons were among those captured before Tsali. Lieutenant Henry Prince, who was assigned to guard the passes in the Great Smoky Mountains and to watch for the fugitives, witnessed the executions of three of Tsali's immediate family on November 23, 1838: "Three of the murderers, George, Jake & Lowan were shot at Camp Scott. They all bore it like philosophers—like plain matters of fact—common sense Indians—Lowan showed no kind of emotion—George's face shone with anxious perspiration—Jake was much troubled."[2]

The army was satisfied that the main culprits in the killings of the soldiers had been executed. On November 24, the soldiers were ordered to leave for Fort Cass. But as they were departing, Euchella's men captured Tsali and executed him on November 25. A witness to Tsali's execution, Jonas Jenkins, said that Tsali asked his executioners to look for the surviving members of his family, after which he calmly and with quiet dignity faced his death. Tsali's youngest son, Wasitu'na or Washington, was spared because of his tender age.[3]

Thomas may have cooperated with the army in the hunt for Tsali's band in order not to jeopardize the position of the Oconaluftee Cherokees. Months earlier, Thomas had negotiated permission for many of the Cherokees in North Carolina to remain in their homeland. Euchella's people were subject to removal because their lands were located inside the boundaries of the Cherokee Nation. They had been hiding in the mountains for several months. In fact, Euchella's wife and son had died of starvation. By aiding the search for Tsali and his family and participating in their capture and execution, Euchella helped secure permission for his people to remain in the East. Colonel William S. Foster, who was charged with locating the "murderers" and gaining satisfaction for the United States, recommended that Euchella's band be allowed to remain in North Carolina with the Oconaluftee Cherokees. In January 1839, the commissioners for the removal of the Cherokees officially agreed.[4]

The story of Tsali was related to James Mooney, an ethnologist who lived among the Cherokees between 1887 and 1890 and during later periods, and to other visitors to the Eastern Band of Cherokees. That story differs in some details from the official records. The two versions are related below.

The first two excerpts are from James Mooney's *Myths of the Cherokees*. They reflect the story as told to him by Tsali's son Washington, the boy who was spared from execution, and by William Holland Thomas and other elderly Cherokees.[5]

The third excerpt is from an official report sent by Lieutenant C. H. Larned to General Winfield Scott explaining the actions of Lieutenant Smith and his men in the Tsali story. Larned ordered Smith to bring some Cherokees from South Carolina to Fort Cass. On the way, they heard of more Cherokees hiding in the mountains. With the guidance of William H. Thomas, they went in search of this other camp. This was Tsali's camp, which included five men and seven women and children. Meanwhile, their original prisoners escaped. Preparing to resume his trip to Fort Cass, Smith returned disarmed rifles to their Cherokee owners and ordered two of his men to give their horses to the women and children. According to Lieutenant Smith, when they resumed their journey, they were attacked by the Indians without warning or provocation. Larned gives his version of how two of his men were killed by Tsali's party and how Tsali's band escaped into the mountains.

The fourth excerpt is a report from Captain John Page to T. Hartley Crawford, commissioner of Indian Affairs, describing the execution of three of the fugitives from Tsali's party.

In the reports made by the soldiers, they claim to have acted toward the women and children of Tsali's band with compassion, which differs from the Cherokee version. Since the soldiers were under orders to treat the Cherokees with consideration, it is highly unlikely they would admit to any unnecessary force that might have provoked Tsali or his family to retaliate. The other details that differ between the versions include the number of soldiers killed and whether Tsali voluntarily turned himself in.[6]

The exact truth will never be known, but the tragedy of Tsali's death at the hands of fellow Cherokees, his brave resistance to forced removal, and the way his death helped secure the freedom of some of the North Carolina Cherokees make this a poignant tragedy.

The story of Tsali, as related to James Mooney by the Cherokees

One old man named Tsalĭ, "Charley," was seized with his wife, his brother, his three sons and their families. Exasperated at the brutality accorded his wife, who, being unable to travel fast, was prodded with bayonets to hasten her steps, he urged the other men to join with him in a dash for liberty. As he spoke in Cherokee the soldiers, although they heard, understood nothing until each warrior suddenly sprang upon the one nearest and endeavored to wrench his gun from him. The attack was so sudden and unexpected that one soldier was killed and the rest fled, while the Indians escaped to the mountains. Hundreds of others, some of them from the various stockades, managed also to escape to the mountains from time to time, where those who did not die of starvation subsisted on roots and wild berries until the hunt was over. Finding it impracticable to secure these fugitives, General Scott finally tendered them a proposition, through (Colonel) W. H. Thomas, their most trusted friend, that if they would surrender Charley and his party for punishment, the rest would be allowed to remain until their case could be adjusted by the government. On hearing of the proposition, Charley voluntarily came in with his sons, offering himself as a sacrifice for his people. By command of General Scott, Charley, his brother, and the two elder sons were shot near the mouth of Tuckasegee, a detachment of Cherokee prisoners being compelled to do the shooting in order to impress upon the Indians the fact of their utter helplessness. From those fugitives thus permitted to remain originated the present eastern band of Cherokee.[7]

The involvement of Euchella, or U'tsălă, in the story of Tsali, as related to James Mooney by the Cherokees

It remains to speak of the eastern band of Cherokee—the remnant which still clings to the woods and waters of the old home country. As has been said, a considerable number had eluded the troops in the general round-up of 1838 and had fled to the fastnesses of the high mountains. Here they were joined by others who had managed to break through the guard at Calhoun and other collecting stations, until the whole number of fugitives in hiding amounted to a thousand or more, principally of the mountain Cherokee of North Carolina, the purest-blooded and most conservative of the Nation. About one-half the refugee warriors had put themselves under command of a noted leader named U'tsălă, "Lichen," who made his headquarters amid the lofty peaks at the head of Oconaluftee, from which secure hiding place, although reduced to extremity of suffering from starvation and exposure, they defied every effort to effect their capture.

The work of running down these fugitives proved to be so difficult an undertaking and so well-nigh barren of result that when Charley and his sons made their bold stroke for freedom General Scott eagerly seized the incident as an opportunity for compromise. To this end he engaged the services of William H. Thomas, a trader who for more than twenty years had been closely identified with the mountain Cherokee and possessed their full confidence, and authorized him to submit to U'tsălă proposition that if the latter would seize Charley and the others who had been concerned in the attack upon the soldiers and surrender them for punishment, the pursuit would be called off and the fugitives allowed to stay unmolested until an effort could be made to secure permission from the general government for them to remain.

Thomas accepted the commission, and taking with him one or two Indians made his way over secret paths to U'tsälä hiding place. He presented Scott's proposition and represented to the chief that by aiding in bringing Charley's party to punishment according to the rules of war he could secure respite for his sorely pressed followers, with the ultimate hope that they might be allowed to remain in their own country, whereas if he rejected the offer the whole force of the seven thousand troops which had now completed the work of gathering up and deporting the rest of the tribe would be set loose upon his own small band until the last refugee had been either taken or killed.

U'tsälä turned the proposition in his mind long and seriously. His heart was bitter, for his wife and little son had starved to death on the mountain side, but he thought of the thousands who were already on their long march into exile and then he looked round upon his little band of followers. If only they might stay, even though a few must be sacrificed, it was better than that all should die—for they had sworn never to leave their country. He consented and Thomas returned to report to General Scott.

Now occurred a remarkable incident which shows the character of Thomas and the masterly influence which he already had over the Indians, although as yet he was hardly more than thirty years old. It was known that Charley and his party were in hiding in a cave of the Great Smokies, at the head of Deep creek, but it was not thought likely that he could be taken without bloodshed and a further delay which might prejudice the whole undertaking. Thomas determined to go to him and try to persuade him to come in and surrender. Declining Scott's offer of an escort, he went alone to the cave, and, getting between the Indians and their guns as they were sitting around the fire near the entrance, he walked up to Charley and announced his message. The old man listened in silence and then said simply, "I will come in. I don't want to be hunted down by my own people." They came in voluntarily and were shot, as has been already narrated, one only, a mere boy, being spared on account of his youth. This boy, now an old man, is still living, Wasitu'na, better known to the whites as Washington.[8]

Excerpt from the report
of First Lieutenant C. H. Larned
to General Winfield Scott

Fort Cass [Charleston], Tenn.
Nov. 5th, 1838

General

. . . Lieut. Smith under the guidance of the W. Thomas . . . came upon the camp of which he went in search and without difficulty or resistance captured twelve Indians, five of whom were men, two of them armed with good rifles; he spent that night at their camp with the intention of going next morning in pursuit of another party, leaving those already taken to be guarded by two of his men: on the morning however an express reached him bearing reiterated orders for his immediate return to this Post and bringing at the same time information of the escape of the prisoners as already stated, he immediately sent back the express with orders for the men from whom the Indians had escaped to return and rejoin him and his march . . . with those whom he had captured, expecting to be joined by the rest of the command before sunset. Having taken off the locks from the two rifles and put them with the powder and ball in charge of a Soldier, he gave the rifles back to the owners to carry, and dismounted two of his men in order to give their horses to the women and children, he proceeded in this manner during the whole day with out perceiving any thing to awaken suspicion until just at sunset, when he observed an Indian carrying a long dirk-knife secreted in his sleeve, he instantly ordered one of his men to take possession of it which was done without the least resistance on the part of the Indian and all went on quietly for a short time when just after passing a laurel branch Lieut. Smith perceived a small axe in the hands of another Indian who walked in front of him close beside the rear man of his party and before the command "take away that axe" could be wholly uttered the weapon was buried in the brain of the Soldier, who fell lifeless beneath the feet of Lieut. Smith's horse, while at the same instant the Corporal in front of the party was mortally wounded by a blow with the butt of a rifle, the third man nearly stunned with a Tomahawk and three Indians seized the Lieut. himself who was enabled to break from their grasp only by the spirit and activity of his horse, which terrified by their yells sprang off instantly at full speed. He was pursued immediately by one of the Indians with the loaded musket taken from the Corporal but only for a short distance, when his persuer returned to the main body and after rifling the dead and wounded men, the whole of them sought refuge in the mountains which rose abruptly from the road. The men for whom Lieut. Smith had sent on the morning came up very soon after and every effort was made to recover some of the Indians, but it was already dark and the mountains into which they had plunged barely practicable by day light, the search therefore was soon discontinued.

The corporal died that night and Lieut. Smith in obedience to the orders which he had received returned immediately to Fort Cass.[9]

Letter from John Page,
captain and principal disbursing agent,
to T. Hartley Crawford,
commissioner of Indian Affairs

Calhoun, Tenn.
4th December, 1838

Sir.

I have the honor to report the arrival of the Troops from the mountains, they having captured the five murderers, four of which were executed, and the fifth was pardoned. The Lufty [Oconaluftee] Indians, that reside in North Carolina rendered great assistence in finding them. After the murderers were caught, —they were tied to trees, the Troops drawn up, and the Lufty Indians shot them. The families of the murderers (nine in number) were brought to this place and will go to the west accompanied by the Troops as prisoners.

I shall endeavor to start the water party this day, John Ross has reported his boat ready.

The Troops will all leave this nation in a [few days]. I shall close up my accounts for the 4th quarter soon as possible.[10]

MURDERED FROM
AN AMBUSH
June 1839

THE LAST OF THIRTEEN detachments of emigrants under the direction of John Ross arrived in the Western Cherokee Nation in late March 1839. The new arrivals, referred to as the "late immigrants," far outnumbered the old settlers and created an integration problem. The late immigrants brought their own government with them. The old settlers were disturbed that the newcomers were not prepared to accept the government already established in the western settlements.[1]

John Ross suggested a council to resolve the problem of integration and to create a union of the old and new settlers. A formal council was convened on June 3, 1839. It took several days for the meetings to get under way. There were speeches from the old settlers and the late immigrants "congratulating each other that they were now reunited as one nation, after having been separated for so long," wrote one observer, the missionary Cephas Washburn. A few of the Treaty Party, including the Ridges, Elias Boudinot, and Stand Watie, had arrived. They soon found they were not welcome. They left the same day, not wanting to cause a disturbance and in fear of their lives.[2]

The congeniality of the council soon deteriorated, when it became apparent that a resolution to the problem of two separate governments would not be easily found. John Brown, principal chief of the old settlers, adjourned the meeting, and the old settlers immediately left the council grounds. The late immigrants remained for two more days at the request of Ross, in order to discuss business related to the emigration.[3]

The failure of the council to resolve many issues among the Treaty Party, the old settlers, and the Ross faction weighed heavily on some of Ross's followers. Rumors grew that the Treaty Party had talked privately with the old settlers to conspire against proposals from Ross at the council. Suspicions of conspiracy amid the continuing grief over the loss of children, wives, and elderly loved ones during the removal worked to create resentment against the Treaty Party. As the council was breaking up, a small group of Ross supporters held a secret council and resolved to invoke the old Blood Law against the leaders of the Treaty Party, whom they held responsible for the deaths of their friends and families. A trial was held for Elias Boudinot, Major Ridge, John Ridge, Stand Watie, James Starr, John Adair Bell, and George W. Adair without the knowledge of any of the accused. Three men from the clans of each of the named defendants sat in judgment of their actions in the implementation of the Treaty of New Echota. All the defendants were condemned to death. A committee planned the executions, and lots were drawn to see who would carry out the sentences.[4]

On the morning of June 22, the first company set out for John Ridge's house. One newspaper account said that the party consisted of forty men, while other accounts estimated that twenty or twenty-five men converged on Ridge's home. The brutal stabbing attack occurred while his family was at home.[5]

Another party was sent to Park Hill, where it waited outside the Reverend Samuel Worcester's house for Elias Boudinot to emerge before approaching the unsuspecting victim and asking for medicine. As Boudinot moved toward the mission house, where the medicines were kept, the assassins pounced, stabbing him and striking him in the head with a tomahawk. Worcester sent a Choctaw who was clearing a new burial ground near the scene of the murder to warn Boudinot's brother Stand Watie, who made a successful escape.[6]

A third party was sent after Major Ridge, who had left the previous day for Van Buren, Arkansas, where one of his slaves lay ill. Learning that Ridge had spent the night in Cincinnati, Arkansas, at the home of Ambrose Harnage, the conspirators set up an ambush nearby. Ten or twelve gunmen shot Ridge from a high precipice as he approached on the road. Some accounts say the shooting took place about ten in the morning, while others say it occurred that evening. A black boy who was accompanying Ridge escaped and carried the news of Ridge's death to nearby settlers, who hurried to the scene to recover the lifeless body.[7]

Friends of the victims immediately suspected John Ross was behind the murders. When Ross sent his brother-in-law to confirm the tragedies, Boudinot's wife, Delight Sargent Boudinot, got word back to Ross that a party was being dispatched to find and kill him in retaliation for the deaths of the Ridges and Boudinot. Ross wrote General Matthew Arbuckle at Fort Gibson appealing for federal troops to intervene for his protection, pending an investigation. The troops weren't needed because several hundred of Ross's supporters surrounded his house to protect him from any potential vengeance attacks. Fearing the gathering of Ross's supporters, and hearing news that more murders had been planned but not yet executed, it was not Ross but

John Adair Bell, Stand Watie, and other Treaty Party leaders who finally sought protection at Fort Gibson.[8]

On July 1, a meeting was held at the Illinois Camp Ground near Tahlequah, the present capital of the Western Cherokee Nation. Members of the Treaty Party were afraid to attend, and most old settlers boycotted the meeting. One of the first actions of the council was to call for amnesty for the murderers of the Ridges and Boudinot. The council asked for all members of the Treaty Party to come forward and publicly confess their error in signing the 1835 treaty, or they would be declared outlaws. Eight did come forward, but the rest, including John Adair Bell and Stand Watie, persisted in their belief that they had negotiated as fair a treaty as possible and had always had the best intentions for their people in all their actions.[9]

The first excerpt below is from a letter written by John Adair Bell and Stand Watie to the *Arkansas Gazette*. It was republished in the *Niles National Register*. The letter describes the deaths of Boudinot and the Ridges. It also gives the views of Bell and Stand Watie on the council convened July 1 calling for them and other Treaty Party members to confess their crimes. The second excerpt is a letter from John Ross to General Matthew Arbuckle describing his reaction to news of Boudinot's death and requesting army protection. Ross was later cleared of complicity in the deaths by witnesses—including his son Allen Ross—who were present at the meeting where the murders were planned.[10]

Excerpt of letter from John Adair Bell and Stand Watie to the *Arkansas Gazette* on the murders of the Ridges and Boudinot

On Saturday of the same week, it being the 22d of June, a party of 20 or 25 Indians proceeded to the house of John Ridge, on Honey creek, in the north part of the Cherokee nation, and having surrounded the house with their rifles, three of them forced his doors, drew him from his bed amidst the screams of his wife and children, and having given him 25 stabs in his body, left him dead in his yard. Maj. Ridge had started on the previous day, to Vineyard, in Washington county, Arkansas. He stayed on Friday night at the house of Mr. Ambrose Harnage, forty miles south of his son's residence. He was waylaid about 10 o'clock on the same morning, by a party of Indians, five miles west of Cane-hill, and shot from a high precipice which commanded the road. It is reported that about 10 or 12 guns were fired at him; only five rifle balls, however, penetrated him body and head. Thus was this aged chief murdered from an ambush, without knowing the dastardly hands who sought his life. This murder occurred in Washington county. About the same hour, four Indians came to Mr. Boudinot, and after a friendly salutation, asked Mr. Boudinot to walk from where his hands were at work, and give them some medicine. Mr. B. who was ever found foremost in acts of charity, obeyed the summons. Shortly after he left the workmen he was struck by these Indians in the back and head, and brought to the earth, with tomahawks, and then stabbed several times in the back with a bowie knife. His head was cleft with the tomahawk in five or six places. These are the circumstances attending the deaths of these individuals.

It is notorious, that although the Ridge's and Boudinot resided at the distance of seventy miles apart, yet report of John Ridge's murder was circulating all through the rank of Ross's party, before B's death was known to his immediate friends. This can perhaps be best explained by the fact that Boudinot and Ross residing about one mile apart. It is equally true that a strong guard were collected around Ross and Gunter [Edward Gunter, a prominent leader of the Ross faction] on the same morning; and Ross has kept a guard of from 200 to 600 persons about his person ever since. It is worthy of remark that Ross promises this guard at the rate of 25 dollars each per month, and gives his due bills to individuals, payable on the faith of the national treasury. These due bills are bought up by his son-in-law and brother with goods. As soon as the undersigned, and some others of the proscribed, could pay the duties of interment to the bodies of their friends, they repaired to Fort Gibson, where they remained for ten days. They there learned upon good authority that they were unsafe while in the power of Ross and his partizans. Since that time they have been generally embodied, for their self-protection.

The convention of John Ross assembled, or rather his guard increased, on the first of July, as anticipated. The subjoined manifesto or decree [giving amnesty to the murderers of the Ridges and Boudinot] will show how far their proceedings were intended to affect the remaining victims of their malice. At the same time these papers were drawn up, a resolution was passed, freely pardoning the murderers of Messrs. Ridges and Boudinot; and all this, too, after Mr. Ross's denial of any knowledge or participation in the matter, and his promise to aid in securing the murderers. Of the documents everyone will judge for himself; but to us they sound very much like the language of an usurper, who first seizes upon the throne, and then requires all the people who have rightly opposed him to swear allegiance to his pretensions. How far the Cherokees west united with the assumptions of Ross and his faction, they will in due time disclose for themselves. If Mr. Ross expects us to purchase our lives by swearing to the infamous oath which he would put in our mouths, he very much mistakes the blood which runs in our veins. Sooner let us fall by the hand of the midnight assassin, than have our names loaded with infamy, and handed down to posterity as traitors, who had "saved their country from total destruction, by making the best treaty ever made for any Indians!" —The historian will do justice to the memories of the fallen. We will never cause their blood to rise in judgment against us, by casting obloquy on their characters. Eight of our friends have abandoned us. [Eight Treaty Party members apologized for signing the treaty in return for amnesty from the Ross faction.] Be the matter with them and their God. We are conscious that we have gained many where we have lost one. The threatened denunciation still hangs over us. Well, if the impending vengeance must fall, let it come upon us with clear consciences.

John A. Bell,
Stand Watie[11]

Letter from John Ross to General Matthew Arbuckle

Park Hill, June 22d 1839

Sir

It has become my painful duty to report to you that I have just heard that Elias Boudinot is killed. Upon receiving intelligence of this unhappy occurrence, I immediately requested my broth[er] in law John G. Ross, who, accompanied by Mr. Lenoir and others, to repair to the place and ascertain the facts, with the view of reporting the same to you. They have returned with a message from Mrs. Boudinot confirming the report with the advice from her, for me to leave home for safety saying that, Stand Waite had determined on raising a company of men for the purpose of coming forthwith to take my life! Why I am thus to be murdered without guilt of any crime—I cannot conceive. Therefore with all due respect, in order that justice may be done, I trust that you will deem it expedient forthwith to interpose and prevent the effusion of innocent blood by exercising your authority, in order that an unbiased investigation might be had in the matter.

Very respectfully I have the honor to be, Sir, yr. obt. Hble. Servt.

Jno Ross[12]

A Citizen of the State of North Carolina
1847 and 1858

During the Creek War, the Cherokees served with the Americans under the command of Andrew Jackson. A group of Cherokees led by Junaluska distinguished themselves at the Battle of Horseshoe Bend in Alabama in 1814 when they swam a river to assist the floundering American army. That action helped Jackson win a decisive battle against the Creeks.[1]

During the 1838 removal, Junaluska was part of the Reverend Jesse Bushyhead's detachment, which made its way west over the northern route, taken by most of the Ross-managed detachments. The detachment had not traveled long when Junaluska led a group of fifty Cherokee escapees. On October 26, 1838, Lieutenant Henry L. Scott wrote General Winfield Scott about the escape:

On my return to this place [Fort Cass at Charleston, Tennessee] I passed Bushyhead's party on Wednesday they were at that time about 13 miles from McMinnville and would reach that place the same day. Mr. Bushyhead informed me that about 50 persons under Chunalusky [Junaluska] a Brother of Wat-chutcha had left him either that morning or on the proceeding day with the declared intention of returning to North Carolina, he stated that the route they would take would be via Kingston & Knoxville and thence join Thomas' Indians. He informed me that he did not use any coercive measures for the purpose of stopping them and that he did not think it his duty so to do. Bushyhead's party deducting these fifty consists of 910 persons and they have with them 50 wagons. He informed me that all the discontented spirits had left his detachment and that he does not anticipate any farther difficulty.[2]

Junaluska and twenty-five other deserters were soon captured near Knoxville, Tennessee. They were taken to Fort Cass, where Junaluska was placed in irons. General Scott wrote that Junaluska would be sent west in chains under guard of the Fourth Infantry, which had been ordered to Fort Gibson in Indian territory to relieve the Seventh Infantry. The Fourth Infantry traveled west by steamboat and train, departing Ross's Landing in mid-December 1838 and arriving at its destination in late January.[3]

Following the forced removal of 1838, small groups of Cherokees made their way back to their old homelands. Even after being sent off in irons, Junaluska returned east. He was reportedly heard to say often after the removal, "If I had known that Jackson would drive us from our homes, I would have killed him that day at the Horseshoe."[4]

In 1847, the North Carolina General Assembly granted Junaluska citizenship and a tract of land in the mountains, in recognition of his service during the Creek War. However, other North Carolina Cherokees had to wait many years for recognition of their citizenship.[5]

In 1858, William Holland Thomas made a speech before the North Carolina Senate in support of a bill to find a residence for Junaluska's widow. Thomas, a senator from Jackson County, took the opportunity to remind his colleagues of the history of the Cherokee Indians in North Carolina. His efforts were intended not only to win a permanent home for Junaluska's widow but for other Cherokees as well. Thomas took a personal interest in the Qualla Cherokees, his relationship with the Indians going back to his youth. Thomas was born near Waynesville, North Carolina, in 1805, his father having died before he was born. He took charge of a trading post frequented by Cherokees when he was only thirteen. The fatherless teenager developed a close relationship with Chief Yonaguska. Thomas soon became involved in many aspects of Cherokee life and political affairs. He spent his entire life as an ardent spokesman for Cherokee interests in North Carolina.[6]

The text of the January 2, 1847, act granting Junaluska citizenship and land is given below. Following that is an excerpt from the speech that Thomas made before the North Carolina Senate in 1858, reminding the members of Junaluska's contributions to the United States and explaining how funds would be used to provide land for his widow in the Cherokee boundary. The excerpt appeared in the *Weekly Standard*.

"An Act in favor of the Cherokee Chief, Junoluskee," as introduced in the North Carolina General Assembly

Whereas the Cherokee Chief Junoluskee, who distinguished himself in the service of the United States at the battle of the "Horse-Shoe," as commander of a body of Cherokees, as well as on divers other occasions during the last war with Great Britain, has, since his removal west of the Mississippi, returned to this State, and expressed a wish to remain and become a citizen thereof:

Sec. 1. *Be it enacted by the General Assembly of the State of North Carolina, and it is hereby enacted by the authority of the same,* That the said Junoluskee be, and he is hereby declared a citizen of the State of North Carolina, and entitled to all the rights, privileges and immunities consequent thereon.

Sec. 2. *Be it further enacted,* That the Secretary of State be, and he is hereby authorised and directed to convey unto the said Junoluskee, in fee simple, the tract of land in Cherokee county, in district 9, tract No. 19, containing three hundred and thirty-seven acres; which said land the said Junoluskee shall be empowered to hold and enjoy, without the power to sell or convey the same, except for the term of two years from time to time: *Provided nevertheless,* that he shall have full power to dispose of the same by devise only.

Sec. 3. *Be it further enacted,* That the Public Treasurer be directed to pay unto the said Junoluskee the sum of one hundred dollars, out of any monies in the treasury not otherwise appropriated.

Sec. 4. *Be it further enacted,* That this act shall be in force from and after its passage.[7]

Excerpt from William Holland Thomas's speech
before the North Carolina Senate,
as printed in the *Weekly Standard*

REMARKS OF MR. THOMAS, Of Jackson

*Delivered in the Senate of North Carolina, on Wednesday, Dec. 1, 1858
on the bill to amend the act of 1783, and to secure to the wife of Junaluska a
residence among the Qualla Town Cherokees, and authorizing the investment
of the proceeds of the sale of the lands owned by her husband, Junaluska, in
lands at that place.*

(Mr. Thomas explained the provisions of the bill, and the
objects designed to be attained by its passage. The reporter has
only deemed it necessary to make a synopsis of the remarks of
Mr. Thomas.)

At the close of the war of the Revolution the resources of
the Colonies having been exhausted, and a permanent peace
with the Indian tribes as well as with Great Britain having become the object of the Federal Government, it was recommended by General Washington to all the States.
North-Carolina, in the recited act of 1783, guaranteed to the
North-Carolina Cherokees the lands claimed by them, with a
permanent residence within the chartered limits of the State,
and secured to them the right of self-government, free from
molestation on the part of the State agreeably to their ancient
usages and customs: and the section of the act which the bill
proposes to repeal subjected the whites to the fine of $200 for
ranging their stock on any land owned by the Indians, and the
informer to have half the sum recovered, besides the forfeiture
of the stock. The Indians do not desire that these penalties
should remain; hence their repeal is provided for. And it is provided further, that upon obtaining the assent of the Indians,
ranging of stock on their mountain lands shall not subject the
stock raisers to the penalties of the law, or the forfeitures of
their stock.

Under the act of 1783, the North-Carolina Cherokees, by taking protection under that act, and by acquiescing in its provisions, ceased to be an independent people; and their permanent residence on the lands of their fathers, endeared to them by the graves and sacred "relics" of their ancestors, did not depend upon their nationality and ability to maintain those rights, but upon the faith of the State, which, by the amendment, it is proposed to preserve and perpetuate.

When the war of 1812 broke out among the Creek Indians, who took sides with Great Britain, the Cherokee Indians, true to their allegiance to the State, took up arms against their brethren, the Creek Indians, and with the whites marched against them, under the command of General Jackson. At the battle of the Horse Shoe the Cherokees were stationed on the opposite side of the river, but as the battle progressed with a prospect of General Jackson and his army being defeated and butchered, Junaluska proposed to his warriors to swim the river and to give aid to their white brethren, by attacking the Creeks in their rear behind the breastworks; this proposition was accepted, and the loud shrill voice of Junaluska as he plunged into the stream was heard, calling on his warriors to follow; soon this little band of Cherokees were seen swimming amid showers of bullets, towards the enemy, and many a warrior sank to rise no more. But on the other bank behind the breastworks is seen the survivors of this little band in deadly conflict with the Creeks, with tomahawk in hand with Junaluska at their head animating his troops. This soon ended the conflict; the Creeks were defeated, and the white army probably saved from defeat and slaughter.

This was followed by peace with the Creeks; and upon the recommendation of General Jackson the government of the United States proposed and concluded the Cherokee treaties of 1817 and 1819, which secured to the heads of Cherokee families the high privilege of becoming citizens of the United States, by the registry of their names with the agent of the tribe.

Junaluska, as well as most of the Cherokees now remaining in North Carolina, availed themselves of this privilege, and had their names enrolled; which, under the decision of the Supreme Court of the State, made in the case of *Euchella vs. Welch*, elevated them to the position of citizens, and threw around them the protection, of the United States; and which rights, with the rights conferred by the State, were provided for and perpetuated by the subsequent acts of the General Assembly and the Cherokee treaties of 1835 and 1846, to which they were not parties. Also, those rights were further sanctioned by the act of Congress of July 29, 1848, and the new policy of the former and present Hon. Secretary of the Interior and the President of the United States, with reference to the Indian tribes located within the States. By this new policy no further encouragement is to be given to the removal of these Indians, but their limits, like the North Carolina Cherokees, were to be circumscribed so as to barely contain a sufficient quantity for their subsistence, for the purpose of encouraging agriculture, the mechanic arts, and civilization among the Indians. To aid in the accomplishment of these objects as the bill proposes, the North Carolina Cherokees reduced their boundary, and within which their ancient usages and customs shall be exercised, and beyond which the laws of the State shall have exclusive jurisdiction over the Indians as well as whites. For these guarantees of protection and permanent residence, the State received the valuable lands acquired of the Cherokees under the treaties of 1817, 1819, and 1833, amounting to several millions of acres.

Under the constitution, those Indians have the right to vote for members of the House of Commons, Governor, members of Congress, and for electors to elect the President and Vice President of the United States; but while permitted within the boundary set apart for their permanent home to be governed by their ancient usages and customs, they will no doubt be content therewith and not interfere with the elections among the whites.

Junaluska, for his meritorious services at the battle of the Horse Shoe, the State by a special act in his favor, conferred upon him all the rights of any other citizen, and also made him a donation of a tract of land in the county of Cherokee for a home for himself and family inalienable except by demise. But Junaluska whose rights, it may be in the remembrance of Senators present, I defended in former days is no more—he has paid the debt of nature, and his widow and children instead of receiving the land donated to Junaluska, is to be sold and the proceeds of the sale invested for their benefit. The bill authorizes the agent to invest the funds within the boundary set apart for the Qualla Town Cherokees, so that they can be among their own people. It would not appear strange to the Senate that some feeling and sympathy were manifested on some occasions when questions relating to those Indians came up in the Senate, when a few of the circumstances which gave rise to them were known. —When an orphan boy we passed over the high mountains which separated the white from the Indian settlement without friend, without money, a pennyless orphan boy, and the North Carolina Cherokees were the first to extend the hand of friendship, ever welcome, but more particularly so with an orphan boy who feels destitute and friendless and the friendship, aid and reciprocal protection that has since existed, and been extended, have completely verified the moral contained in Esop's fable of the Lion and the mouse, and taught him the useful lesson never to betray or desert a friend, the red as well as the white, the poor and persecuted as well as the more favorably situated.[8]

IF NOT REJOICING,
AT LEAST IN COMFORT
1864

WINFIELD SCOTT was the quintessential soldier. He joined the military when he was twenty-two and stayed for over fifty years. Recognized by his superiors for his leadership during the War of 1812, he was promoted to the rank of brigadier general at the young age of twenty-seven. In 1832, he fought in the Black Hawk War, which came about when hostilities broke out between the Indians and frontier settlers on the upper Mississippi. He was sent to the Seminole War in 1835 to lead the American forces and later served in the Mexican War. In 1852, he ran for president but lost to Franklin Pierce. He retired from military duty on October 31, 1861.[1]

During the War of 1812, Scott became good friends with Martin Van Buren.[2] When Van Buren was faced with implementing President Jackson's Indian removal policies, he called on his old friend Scott to carry out the final steps of the forced removal.

Over the course of the Cherokee Removal and many years later while writing his memoirs, Scott seemed to be in denial about the terrible loss of life caused by illness and about the hardships faced by the Cherokees uprooted from their homes and sent west. His reports to Secretary of War Joel R. Poinsett during the removal presented the whole process in the best possible light. "The troops and Indians, in all their camps, continue to enjoy good general health," he wrote. It is ironic that he denied not only the illnesses of the Cherokees but of his own troops, for in the same letter Scott complained that "my own health [is] seriously affected by a transition (without a season between) from the snows of the north into the torrid heat of a southern summer." He also reported that Colonel William Lindsay was "sick and absent."[3] The terrible heat, drought, and unsanitary closeness of the camps—including the military camps—affected everyone.

The *Memoirs of Lieut.-General Scott, LL.D.: Written by Himself* were published in 1864. Scott began the journal in the first person, then changed to the third person, referring to himself as "the autobiographer," "Lt. Colonel Scott," or simply "Scott." He wrote in his memoirs that "war is the normal or natural state of man."[4]

Below is one continuous passage from Scott's memoirs. In it, he describes the Cherokee Removal from his perspective and includes excerpts from some of the orders he issued during the removal. The first such excerpt is from Removal Order No. 25. The full text of that order is included in this book as Appendix 2.

Excerpt from the
Memoirs of Lieut.-General Scott, LL.D.: Written by Himself

The frontiers being for the time quieted by the means narrated, by the thaw of the spring, and the return of the farming season of industry, Scott was called to Washington and ordered thence to the Southwest—charged with the delicate duty of removing the Cherokee Indians, under certain treaty stipulations, to their new country on the upper Arkansas River. This work unavoidably fell upon the military, and with *carte blanche*, from President Van Buren, under his sign manual—Mr. Secretary Poinsett being very ill—Scott undertook the painful duty—with the firm resolve that it should be done judiciously, if possible, and, certainly, in mercy.

The number of volunteers called for by Scott's predecessor (Colonel Lindsay) in that special command, independent of a few regulars, was overwhelming. Hence resistance on the part of the Indians would have been madness. The Cherokees were an interesting people—the greater number Christians, and many as civilized as their neighbors of the white race. Between the two colors intermarriages had been frequent. They occupied a contiguous territory—healthy mountains, valleys, and plains lying in North Carolina, Georgia, Alabama, and Tennessee. Most of their leading men had received good educations, and possessed much ability. Some were quite wealthy in cultivated farms, good houses, cattle of every kind, and *negro slaves*. Gardens and orchards were seen everywhere, and the women graceful, with, in many cases, added beauty. Of course the mixed races are here particularly alluded to. The mountaineers were still wild men, but little on this side of their primordial condition.

The North Carolinians and Tennesseans were kindly disposed toward their red brethren. The Alabamians much less so. The great difficulty was with the Georgians (more than half the army), between whom and the Cherokees there had been feuds and wars for many generations. The reciprocal hatred of the two races was probably never surpassed. Almost every Georgian, on leaving home, as well as after arrival at New Echota, —the centre of the most populous district of the Indian territory—vowed never to return without having killed at least one

Indian. This ferocious language was the more remarkable as the great body of these citizens—perhaps, seven in ten—were professors of religion. The Methodist, Baptist, and other ministers of the Gospel of Mercy, had been extensively abroad among them; but the hereditary animosity alluded to caused the Georgians to forget, or, at least, to deny, that a Cherokee was a human being. It was, however, to that general religious feeling which Scott had witnessed in the Georgia troops, both in Florida and on the Chattahoochee in 1836, that he now meant to appeal, and on which he placed his hopes of avoiding murder and other atrocities. And as will be seen that blessed sentiment responded.

The autobiographer arrived at the Cherokee Agency, a small village on the Hiawassee, within the edge of Tennessee, early in May, 1838, and published the subjoined addresses to the troops and Indians. Both were printed at the neighboring village, Athens, and to show singleness of feeling and policy, the two papers were very extensively circulated *together*, among all concerned.

"Extracts from General Orders, or the Address to the Troops

"Headquarters, Eastern Division, Cherokee Agency, May 17, 1838

"Considering the number and temper of the mass to be removed, together with the extent and fastnesses of the country occupied, it will readily occur that simple indiscretions, acts of harshness and cruelty on the part of our troops may lead, step by step, to delays, to impatience, and exasperation, and, in the end, to a general war and carnage—a result, *in the case of these particular Indians, utterly abhorrent to the generous sympathies of the whole American people*. Every possible kindness, compatible with the necessity of removal must therefore, be shown by the troops; and if, in the ranks, a despicable individual should be found capable of inflicting a wanton injury or insult on any Cherokee man, woman, or child, it is hereby made the special duty of the nearest good officer or man instantly to interpose, and to seize and consign the guilty wretch to the severest penalty of the laws. The major-general is fully persuaded that this injunction will not be neglected by the brave men under his command, who cannot be otherwise than jealous of their own honor and that of their country.

"By early and persevering acts of kindness and humanity, it is impossible to doubt that the Indians may soon be induced to confide in the army, and, instead of fleeing to mountains and forests, flock to us for food and clothing. If, however, through false apprehensions, individuals, or a party here and there, should seek to hide themselves, they must be pursued and invited to surrender, but not fired upon, unless they should make a stand to resist. Even in such cases, mild remedies may sometimes better succeed than violence; and it cannot be doubted, if we get possession of the women and children first, or first capture the men, that, in either case, the outstanding members of the same families will readily come in on the assurance of forgiveness and kind treatment.

"Every captured man, as well as all who surrender themselves, must be disarmed, with the assurance that their weapons will be carefully preserved and restored at, or beyond the Mississippi. In either case, the men will be guarded and escorted, except it may be where their women and children are safely secured as hostages; but, in general families in our possession will not be separated, unless it be to send men, as runners, to invite others to come in.

"It may happen that Indians will be found too sick, in the opinion of the nearest surgeon, to be removed to one of the depots indicated above. In every such case, one or more of the family or the friends of the sick person will be left in attendance, with ample subsistence and remedies, and the remainder of the family removed by the troops. Infants, superannuated persons, lunatics, and women in helpless condition, will all, in the removal, require peculiar attention, which the brave and humane will seek to adapt to the necessities of the several cases."

"Major-General Scott, of the United States' Army, sends to the Cherokee people remaining in North Carolina, Georgia, Tennessee, and Alabama this Address

"Cherokees: —The President of the United States has sent me, with a powerful army, to cause you, in obedience to the treaty of 1835, to join that part of your people who are already established in prosperity on the other side of the Mississippi. Unhappily, the two years which were allowed for the purpose, you have suffered to pass away without following, and without making any preparation to follow, and now, or by the time that this solemn *address* shall reach your distant settlements, the emigration must be commenced in haste, but, I hope, without disorder. I have no power, by granting a farther delay, to correct the error that you have committed. The full moon of May is already on the wane, and before another shall have passed away, every Cherokee man, woman, and child, in those States, must be in motion to join their brethren in the far West.

"My friends—This is no, sudden determination on the part of the President whom you and I must now obey. By the treaty, the emigration was to have been completed on or before the 23d of this month, and the President has constantly kept you warned, during the two years allowed, through all his officers and agents in this country, that the treaty would be enforced.

"I am come to carry out that determination. My troops already occupy many positions in the country that you are to abandon, and thousands and thousands are approaching from every quarter to render resistance and escape alike hopeless.

All those troops, regular and militia, are your friends. Receive them and confide in them as such. Obey them when they tell you that you can remain no longer in this country. Soldiers are as kind-hearted as brave, and the desire of every one of us is to execute our painful duty in mercy. We are commanded by the President to act toward you in that spirit, and such is also the wish of the whole people of America.

"Chiefs, head men, and warriors—Will you then, by resistance, compel us to resort to arms? God forbid! Or will you, by flight, seek to hide yourselves in mountains and forests, and thus oblige us to hunt you down? Remember that, in pursuit it may be impossible to avoid conflicts. The blood of the white man, or the blood of the red man, may be spilt, and if spilt, however accidentally, it may be impossible for the discreet and humane among you, or among us, to prevent a general war and carnage. Think of this, my Cherokee brethren! I am an old warrior, and have been present at many a scene of slaughter; but spare me, I beseech you, the horror of witnessing the destruction of the Cherokees.

"Do not, I invite you, even wait for the close approach of the troops; but make such preparations for emigration as you can, and hasten to this place, to Ross's Landing, or to Gunter's Landing, where you will all be received in kindness by officers selected for the purpose. You will find food for all, and clothing for the destitute, at either of those places, and thence at your case, and in comfort, be transported to your new homes according to the terms of the treaty.

"This is the address of a warrior to warriors. May his entreaties be kindly received, and may the God of both prosper the Americans and Cherokees, and preserve them long in peace and friendship with each other.

"WINFIELD SCOTT"

There was some delay in bringing in the mountaineers of North Carolina; but most of the people residing in Tennessee and Alabama were readily collected for emigration. Scott remained with the Georgians, and followed up his printed addresses by innumerable lessons and entreaties.

The latter troops commenced in their own State the collection of the Indians, with their movable effects, May 26. Scott looked on in painful anxiety. Food in abundance had been provided at the depots, and wagons accompanied every detachment of troops. The Georgians distinguished themselves by their humanity and tenderness. Before the first night thousands—men, women, and children—sick and well were brought in. Poor creatures! They had obstinately refused to prepare for the removal. Many arrived half-starved, but refused the food that was pressed upon them. At length, the children, with less pride, gave way, and next their parents. The Georgians were the waiters on the occasion—many of them with flowing tears. The autobiographer has never witnessed a scene of deeper pathos.

Some cheerfulness, after awhile, began to show itself, when, counting noses, one family found that a child, another an aged aunt, etc. had been left behind. Instantly dozens of the volunteers asked for wagons, or saddle horses, with guides, to bring in the missing.

In a few days, without shedding a drop of blood, the Indians, with the exception of small fragments were collected—those of North Carolina, Georgia, and Tennessee at the Agency, in, a camp twelve miles by four; well shaded, watered with perennial springs, and flanked by the Hiawassee. The *locale* was happily chosen, as a most distressing drought of some four months—counting from about the middle of June—came upon the whole Southwestern country, that stopped any movement to the West till November; for the Tennessee, Mississippi, and Arkansas Rivers ceased to be navigable by the beginning of July; and on the land route, to the Arkansas, there were many spaces of twenty, forty, and even sixty, miles, without sufficient water for the inhabitants and their cattle. The other camps of emigration were also shaded and watered. Scott caused the few sick to be well attended by good physicians; all proper subjects to be vaccinated; rode through the principal camp almost daily, and having placed the emigration in the hands of the Cherokee authorities themselves—after winning the confidence of all—was at liberty, at an early day, to the great benefit of the treasury, to send all the volunteers to their respective homes, except a single company. A regiment of regulars, to meet contingencies, was also retained. Two others were despatched to Florida and the Canada frontiers. The company of volunteers (Tennesseeans) were a body of respectable citizens, and under their judicious commander, Captain Robertson, of great value as a police force. The Cherokees were receiving from Government immense sums; as fast as decreed by a civil commission (then in session) in the way of damages and indemnities, which attracted swarms of gamblers, sleight-of-hand men, blacklegs, and other desperadoes. The camp was kept cleansed of all such vermin by the military police—a duty which, probably, would have been resisted if it had devolved on regular troops.

At length, late in October rain began to fall and the rivulets to flow. In a week or two, the rivers were again navigable. All were prepared for the exodus. Power had said:

"There lies your way, due West."

And a whole people now responded:

"Then Westward—ho!"

They took their way, if not rejoicing, at least in comfort.

"Some natural tears they dropt, but wiped them soon."

Many of the miseries of life they had experienced; but hope—a worldly, as well as a Christian's hope, cheered them on. Scott followed up the movement nearly to the junction of the Ohio and Mississippi, where he gave his parting blessing to a people who had long shared his affectionate cares. He has reason to believe that, on the whole, their condition has been improved by transportation.[5]

Appendix 1
Guide to Cherokee Detachments, 1837–39

"Voluntary" Enrollments and Removals

1. About January 1, 1837, some 600 Treaty Party members left under their own management, accompanied by their Negro slaves and livestock. They traveled through Tennessee, Kentucky, Illinois, Missouri, and Arkansas. No deaths were reported.

2. On March 3, 1837, some 466 Treaty Party members left Ross's Landing, Tennessee, in a fleet of 11 flatboats moving in 3 groups. The detachment included Major Ridge and his family and was conducted by Dr. John S. Young. A total of 4 deaths were reported. The party arrived in the West on March 28, 1837.

3. On October 13, 1837, some 365 Treaty Party members left from Charleston, Tennessee, traveling the northern route. The detachment was conducted by B. B. Cannon. A total of 15 deaths were reported. The party arrived in the West on December 28, 1837.

4. On April 5, 1838, some 250 volunteers left by water from Ross's Landing. The conductor was Lieutenant Edward Deas, who took charge at Waterloo, Alabama. A total of 2 deaths were reported. When the party arrived in the West on May 1, 1838, it included a reported 248 persons.

Forced, Military-led Detachments

5. On June 6, 1838, some 800 people were forced on to 6 flat-boats pulled by a steamboat at Ross's Landing. The conductor was Lieutenant Edward Deas. No deaths were reported. When the party arrived in the West on June 20, 1838, it included a reported 489 persons.

6. On June 12 or 15, 1838, some 876 people were forced on to flatboats hauled by steamboat at Ross's Landing. The conductor was Lieutenant R. H. K. Whitely. Some 70 or 73 deaths were reported. The detachment arrived in the West on August 5, 1838.

7. On June 17, 1838, some 1,071 or 1,072 people left Ross's Landing. They traveled by wagon train to Waterloo, Alabama, then by water. Captain G. S. Drane joined the detachment at Bellefonte, Alabama, and served as conductor. A total of 146 deaths, 293 desertions, and 2 births were reported. The party arrived in the West on September 7, 1838.

Ross-managed Detachments

8. A party of 858 people left on September 1, 1838, and re-started in early October 1838. It departed from Gunstocker Creek and traveled the northern route. The conductor was Elijah Hicks, and the assistant conductor was White Path. A total of 5 births and 34 deaths were reported, including White Path. When the party arrived in the West on January 4, 1839, it included a reported 744 persons.

9. A party of 729 people left on August 28, 1838, and restarted in early October 1838. It departed from near Charleston on the northern route. The conductor was Hair Conrad, who was

replaced by assistant conductor Daniel Colston after Conrad became ill. A total of 54 deaths, 9 births, and 24 desertions were reported. When the party arrived in the West on January 16 or 17, 1839, it included a reported 654 persons.

10. On October 4 or 10, 1838, some 1,200 people left from Fort Payne, Alabama, by the southern route. The conductor was John Benge, and the assistant conductor was George C. Lowrey. A total of 33 deaths and 3 births were reported. When the party arrived in the West on January 11, 1839, it included a reported 1,132 persons.

11. In October 1838, some 950 people left from the Chatata Creek area by the northern route. The conductor was Jesse Bushyhead, and the assistant conductor was Roman Nose. A total of 38 deaths, 6 births, and 148 desertions were reported. When the party arrived in the West on February 27, 1839, it included a reported 898 persons.

12. In October 1838, some 1,250 people left from Charleston by the northern route. The conductor was Situwakee, and the assistant conductor was the Reverend Evan Jones. A total of 71 deaths and 5 births were reported. When the party arrived in the West on February 2, 1839, it included a reported 1,033 persons.

13. In October 1838, some 983 people left from Candy's Creek near Cleveland by the northern route. The conductor was Old Fields, and the assistant conductor was Stephen Foreman. A total of 57 deaths and 17 or 19 births were reported. When the party arrived in the West on February 23 or 27, 1839, it included a reported 921 persons.

14. In October 1838, some 1,035 people left from the Charleston area by the northern route. The conductor was Moses Daniel,

and the assistant conductor was George Still. A total of 48 deaths and 6 births were reported. When the party arrived in the West on March 2, 1839, it included a reported 924 persons.

15. In October 1838, some 1,150 people left the Mouse Creek area by the northern route. The conductor was Choowalooka, and the assistant conductor was J. D. Wofford. Wofford was dismissed at Willard's Ferry on the Mississippi River. No deaths were reported, though this is questionable. When the party arrived in the West on March 1, 1839, it included a reported 970 persons.

16. On October 26, 1838, some 850 people left Vann's Town near Harrison, Tennessee. They traveled to McMinnville, then joined the northern route. The conductor was James Brown, and the assistant conductor was Lewis Hilderbrand. A total of 34 deaths and 3 births were reported. When the party arrived in the West on March 5, 1839, it included a reported 717 persons.

17. In late October or on November 4, 1838, some 1,118 people left the Mouse Creek area by the northern route. The conductor was George Hicks, and the assistant conductor was Collins McDonald. No deaths were reported, though this is questionable. When the party arrived in the West on March 14, 1839, it included a reported 1,039 persons.

18. On November 1 or 6, 1838, some 1,029 people left Vann's Town and followed the same route as the party led by James Brown. The conductor was Richard Taylor, and the assistant conductor was W. S. Adair. A total of 55 deaths and 15 births were reported. When the detachment arrived in the West on March 24, 1839, it included a reported 942 or 944 persons.

19. On November 7, 1838, some 1,766 people left from the

Charleston area by the northern route. The conductor was Peter Hilderbrand, and the assistant conductor was James Hilderbrand. No deaths were officially reported, though unofficial reports say 55 persons died. When the party arrived in the West on March 25, 1839, it included a reported 1,312 members.

20. On December 5, 1838, some 231 people left Charleston by boat. The conductor was John Drew, and the assistant conductor was John Golden Ross, John Ross's brother-in-law. A total of 12 deaths were reported, including Quatie, John Ross's wife. When the party arrived in the West on March 18, 1839, it included a reported 219 persons.

Military-led Treaty Party Detachment

21. On October 11, 1838, some 660 people left from Charleston. They traveled to Ross's Landing and Memphis by land, then on to Oklahoma. The military conductor was Lieutenant Edward Deas, the Cherokee conductor was John Adair Bell, and the assistant conductor was David L. Walker. A total of 23 deaths were reported. The party arrived in the West on January 7, 1839.

Prisoners of the Fourth United States Infantry

22. On December 12, 1838, some 25 prisoners, including Junaluska, left Charleston under guard of the Fourth Infantry. They traveled overland to Kelly's Ferry on the Tennessee River, then took steamboats. They arrived in the West in late January 1839.

Editor's note: This list of detachments should be used only as a guide. The sources consulted in compiling it contain discrepancies.[1]

Appendix 2
General Winfield Scott's
Removal Order No. 25

Head Quarters, Eastern Division.
Cherokee Agency, Ten. May 17, 1838.

MAJOR GENERAL SCOTT, of the United States' Army, announces to the troops assembled and assembling in this country, that, with them, he has been charged by the President to cause the Cherokee Indians yet remaining in North Carolina, Georgia, Tennessee and Alabama, to remove to the West, according to the terms of Treaty of 1835. His Staff will be as follows:

Lieutenant Colonel W. J. Worth, acting Adjutant General, Chief of the Staff
Major M. M. Payne, acting Inspector General
Lieutenants R. Anderson, & E. D. Keyes, regular Aids-de-camp
Colonel A. H. Kenan & Lieutenant H. B. Shaw, volunteer Aids-de-camp

Any order given orally, or in writing, by either of those officers, in the name of the Major General will be respected and obeyed as if given by himself.

The Chiefs of Ordnance, of the Quarter-Master's Department and of the Commissariat, as also the Medical Director of this Army, will, as soon as they can be ascertained, be announced in orders.

To carry out the general object with the greatest promptitude and certainty, and with the least possible distress to the Indians, the country they are to evacuate is divided into three principal Military Districts, under as many officers of high rank, to command the troops serving therein, subject to the instructions of the Major General.

Eastern District, to be commanded by Brigadier General Eustis, of the United States' Army or the highest officer in rank, serving therein: —North Carolina, the part of Tennessee lying north of Gilmer county, Georgia and the counties of Gilmer, Union, and Lumpkin, in Georgia. Head Quarters, in the first instance, say, at Fort Butler.

Western District, to be commanded by Colonel Lindsay, of the United States' Army, or the highest officer in rank serving therein: —Alabama, the residue of Tennessee and Dade county, in Georgia. Head quarters, in the first instance, say, at Ross' Landing.

Middle District, to be commanded by Brigadier General Armistead of the United States' Army, or the highest officer in rank serving therein: —All that part of the Cherokee country, lying within the State of Georgia, and which is not comprised in the two other districts. Head Quarters, in the first instance, say, at New Echota.

It is not intended that the foregoing boundaries between the principal commanders shall be strictly observed. Either, when carried near the district of another, will not hesitate to extend his operations, according to the necessities of the case, but with all practicable harmony, in the adjoining district. And, among his principal objects, in case of actual or apprehended hostilities, will be that of affording adequate protection to our white people in and around the Cherokee country.

The senior officer actually present in each district will receive instructions from the Major General as to the time of commencing the removal, and every thing that may occur interesting to the service, in the district, will be promptly reported to the same source. The Major General will endeavour to visit in a short time all parts of the Cherokee country occupied by the troops.

The duties devolved on the army, through the orders of the Major General & those of the commanders of districts, under him, are of a highly important and critical nature.

The Cherokees, by the advances which they have made in christianity and civilization, are by far the most interesting tribe of Indians in the territorial limits of the United States. Of the 15,000 of those people who are now to be removed—(and the time within which a voluntary emigration was stipulated, will expire on the 23rd instant—) it is understood that about four fifths are opposed, or have become averse to a distant emigration; and altho' none are in actual hostilities with the United States, or threaten a resistance by arms, yet the troops will probably be obliged to cover the whole country they inhabit, in order to make prisoners and to march or to transport the prisoners, by families, either to this place, to Ross' Landing or Gunter's Landing, where they are to be finally delivered over to the Superintendant of Cherokee Emigration.

Considering the number and temper of the mass to be removed, together with the extent and fastnesses [vastness] of the country occupied, it will readily occur, that simple indiscretions—acts of harshness and cruelty, on the part of our troops, may lead, step by step, to delays, to impatience and exasperation, and in the end, to a general war and carnage—a result, in the case of those particular Indians, utterly abhorrent to the generous sympathies of the whole American people. Every possible kindness, compatible with the necessity of removal, must, therefore, be shown by the troops, and, if, in the ranks, a despicable individual should be found, capable of inflicting a wanton injury or insult on any Cherokee man, woman or child, it is hereby made the special duty of the nearest good officer or man, instantly to interpose, and to seize and consign the guilty wretch to the severest penalty of the laws. The Major General is fully persuaded that this injunction will not be neglected by the brave men under his command, who cannot be otherwise than jealous of the own honor and that of their country.

By early and persevering acts of kindness and humanity, it is impossible to doubt that the Indians may soon be induced to confide in the Army, and instead of fleeing to mountains and forests, flock to us for food and clothing. If, however, through false apprehensions, individuals, or a party, here and there, should seek to hide themselves, they must be pursued and invited to surrender, but not fired upon unless they should make a stand to resist. Even in such cases, mild remedies may sometimes better succeed than violence; and it cannot be doubted that if we get possession of the women and children first, or first capture the men, that, in either case, the outstanding members of the same families will readily come in on the assurance of forgiveness and kind treatment.

Every captured man, as well as all who surrender themselves, must be disarmed, with the assurance that their weapons will be carefully preserved and restored at, or beyond the Mississippi. In either case, the men will be guarded and escorted, except it may be, where their women and children are safely secured as hostages; but, in general, families, in our possession, will not be separated, unless it be to send men, as runners, to invite others to come in.

It may happen that the Indians will be found too sick, in the opinion of the nearest Surgeon, to be removed to one of the depots indicated above. In every such case, one or more of the family, or the friends of the sick person, will be left in attendance, with ample subsistence and remedies, and the remainder of the family removed by the troops. Infants, superannuated persons, lunatics and women in a helpless condition, will all, in the removal, require peculiar attention, which the brave and humane will seek to adapt to the necessities of the several cases.

All strong men, women, boys & girls, will be made to march under proper escorts. For the feeble, Indian horses and ponies will furnish a ready resource, as well as for bedding and light cooking utensils—all of which, as intimated in the Treaty, will be necessary to the emigrants both in going to, and after arrival at, their new homes. Such, and all other light articles of property, the Indians, will be allowed to collect and to take with them, as also their slaves, who will be treated in like manner with the Indians themselves.

If the horses and ponies be not adequate to the above purposes, wagons must be supplied.

Corn, oats, fodder and other forage, also beef cattle, belonging to the Indians to be removed, will be taken possession of by the proper departments of the Staff, as wanted, for the regular consumption of the Army, and certificates given to the owners, specifying in every case, the amount of forage and the weight of beef, so taken, in order that the owners may be paid for the same on their arrival at one of the depots mentioned above.

All other moveable or personal property, left or abandoned by the Indians, will be collected by agents appointed for the purpose, by the Superintendant of Cherokee Emigration, under a system of accountability, for the benefit of the Indian owners, which he will devise. The army will give to those agents, in their operations, all reasonable countenance, aid and support.

White men and widows, citizens of the United States, who are, or have been intermarried with Indians, and thence commonly termed, *Indian countrymen;* also such Indians as have been made denizens of particular States by special legislation, together with the families and property of all such persons, will not be molested or removed by the troops until a decision, on the principles involved, can be obtained from the War Department.

A like indulgence, but only for a limited time, and until

further orders, is extended to the families and property of certain Chiefs and head-men of the two great Indian parties, (on the subject of emigration) now understood to be absent in the direction of Washington on the business of their respective parties.

This order will be carefully read at the head of every company in the Army.[1]

By Command:

Winfield Scott
W. J. Worth, Chief of the Staff[1]

Appendix 3

General Winfield Scott's

Removal Order No. 62

Head Quarters Eastern Division
Cherokee Agency, July 5, 1838

The Indians now encamped near Red Clay and Cleveland will be immediately concentrated at or within a mile around the old Indian Camp ground about 12 miles from this place, on the road to Red Clay.

Lt. Colo. Hunter and Captain Vernon will each with all his troops, accompany the Indians to their new camp where the mounted company will proceed to this place in time to be honourably discharged and paid off on the day its term of service expires.

Lieut. Colo. Hunter and battalion will, for a time, take post at the new Indian Camp.

As soon as the Indians shall be established in their new camp, the Indian Department will charge itself with their subsistence and medical care.

The Quarter Master and Commissary here, will immediately take measures to remove, or to dispose of the public property at Red Clay, Cleveland, and for the subsistence of the battalion that is to be temporarily stationed at the Indian Camp. They will also give the necessary attention to the public property at Fort Morrow, which post is about to be abandoned.

Captain Morrow will march his Company to this place for

an honourable discharge and payment at the close of its term of service.

By Command of Major Gen. Scott
Robert Anderson Lt.[1]

APPENDIX 4
GENERAL WINFIELD SCOTT'S CIRCULAR TO CHEROKEE CONDUCTORS

Head qua. Eastern Division
Cherokee Agency Oct. 4, 1838

Sir:

Writing in reply to a suggestion made to me by the war department that it might be necessary to send a guard of soldiers with each detachment of Cherokee emigrants, moving by land, I said to the honourable Secretary, August the 3d, as follows: —

"Those agents (the Cherokee delegation) do not deem a military escort necessary for the *protection* of the emigrants on the route, nor do I. We are equally of the opinion that sympathy and kind offices will be very generally shown to the emigrants, by the citizens, throughout the movement, & the Indians are desirous to exhibit, in return, the orderly habits which their acquired civilization has conferred. The parties, of about 1,000 each, will march without (or with but few) arms, under Indian conductors & sub-officers—all of intelligence & discretion, who are ready to promise to repress & to punish all disorders among their own people, & if they commit outrages on the citizens, or depredations on their property, instantly to deliver the offenders over to the nearest civil officers of the states. I have full confidence in their promises & capacity to do all that they are ready to undertake."

Since the 3d of August nothing has occurred to change the

good opinion, then entertained, of the Cherokee people, [and] it is sincerely hoped that their conduct on the road will fully sustain that opinion. Hence it has not yet been thought necessary to appoint a guard to accommpany any detachment of emigrants & I am now anxiously waiting to learn whether the first, second and third detachments conduct themselves as well on the road as I have hoped and expected.

A copy of this *Circular* will be sent or given to the conductor of every detachment of emigrants for the information & government of all concerned.

Wishing you & your people, comfort & expedition on the road with all prosperity in your new country, I remain truly,

The friend of the Cherokees,
Winfield Scott

To: Mr. _____
Conductor of a Detachment of Cherokee Emigrants[1]

Appendix 5
General John E. Wool's
General Order No. 74

HEAD QUARTERS, ARMY E.T. & C.N. FORT CASS, November 3d, 1836

I am instructed by the President of the United States, through the War Department, to make known to Mr. John Ross, and all others whom it may concern, that it is his determination to have the late Treaty, entered into between the United States and the Cherokee People, and ratified by the Senate, the 25th May, 1836, "religiously fulfilled in all its parts, terms and conditions, within the period prescribed," and that "no delegation which may be sent" to Washington "with a view to obtain new terms, or a modification of those of the existing treaty, will be received or recognized, nor will any intercourse be had with them, directly or indirectly, orally or in writing;" and that the President regards the proceedings of Mr. Ross and his associates in the late Council held at Red Clay, "as in direct contravention of the plighted faith of their people, and a repetition of them will be considered as indicative of a design to prevent the execution of the Treaty, even at the hazard of actual hostilities, and they will be promptly repressed."

It is further made known by instructions from the War Department, that "if any of our citizens enter the Cherokee country and incite opposition to the execution of the treaty," they will be proceeded against according to the laws of the State, if any exist on the subject, in which they may enter; and if there should be "no law of the State which can be brought to bear on them, and under which that may be removed," "it is the opinion of the President" as expressed through the War Department "that they may be removed" out of the country, "under the 6th article of the treaty," in which the United States guarantee that the Cherokees shall be "protected against interruption and intrusion from citizens of the United States who may attempt to settle in the country," unless it is with the express consent "of the Committee who are acting under the 12th Article of the Treaty, and by the terms of the Article they alone are authorized to give it."

All officers of the Army, whether commanding Volunteers or Regular Troops, under my command, are required and directed to make known to all persons residing, or who may come within the range of their respective commands, the contents of this order. And to make diligent search and enquiry in regard to all citizens who may enter the Cherokee country, and incite opposition or interfere with the due execution of the treaty, and report their names and places of residence without delay, to General Head Quarters, in order that they may be proceeded against, according to the laws of the country, and the instructions of the President of the United States. They are also required and directed to prevent all meetings and to break up all Councils coming to their knowledge, assembled in the Cherokee country, for the purpose of opposing the treaty, or discussing its non-execution.

John E. Wool
Brig. Gen'l
Comdg.[1]

Endnotes

Introduction

1. Elias Boudinot, "Indian's Sorrow," *Cherokee Phoenix*, 27 March 1828: 2.
2. Theda Perdue and Michael D. Green, eds. *The Cherokee Removal: A Brief History with Documents* (Boston and New York: Bedford Books of St. Martin's Press, 1995), 13-14, 50, 52-57, 59, 75.
3. Ronald N. Satz, *American Indian Policy in the Jacksonian Era* (Lincoln: University of Nebraska Press, 1975), 15, 19.
4. Satz, *American Indian Policy*, 3; Perdue and Green, *Cherokee Removal*, 58.
5. Althea Bass, *Cherokee Messenger*, 1936 (reprint, Norman and London: University of Oklahoma Press, 1996), 108; William L. Anderson, ed., *Cherokee Removal: Before and After* (Athens and London: University of Georgia Press, 1991), ix.
6. Russell Thornton, "The Demography of the Trail of Tears Period: A New Estimate of Cherokee Population Losses," *Cherokee Removal: Before and After*, William L. Anderson, ed. (Athens and London: University of Georgia Press, 1991), 75.
7. Satz, *American Indian Policy*, 4-6.
8. Satz, *American Indian Policy*, 3,11; Bass, *Cherokee Messenger*, 109-10.

9. Satz, *American Indian Policy*, 17; Jeremiah Evarts, *Cherokee Removal: The William Penn Essays and Other Writings*, Francis Paul Prucha, ed. and intro. (Knoxville: University of Tennessee Press, 1981), 43-306; *Cherokee Phoenix and Indians' Advocate*, 28 Oct. 1829.

10. Satz, *American Indian Policy*, 23, 30; *Speeches on the Passage of the Bill for the Removal of the Indians, Delivered in the Congress of the United States, April and May 1830* (Boston: Perkins and Marvin; New York: Jonathan Leavitt, 1830), 69-78.

11. *Speeches on the Passage*, 251; Thurman Wilkins, *Cherokee Tragedy: The Story of the Ridge Family and the Decimation of a People*, 1970 (2d ed., Norman and London: University of Oklahoma Press, 1986), 219.

12. Satz, *American Indian Policy*, 29, 34-35.

13. Ibid., 29.

14. Ibid., 30.

15. Ibid., 9, 32-33.

16. Ibid., 9, 30.

17. Bass, *Cherokee Messenger*, 113, 114.

18. Theda Perdue, "The Conflict Within," *Cherokee Removal: Before and After*, William L. Anderson, ed. (Athens and London: University of Georgia Press, 1991), 70-71.

19. Wilkins, *Cherokee Tragedy*, 225-26, 227; Bass, *Cherokee Messenger*, 129-50; Samuel A. Worcester, "Mr. Worcester's Account of His Second Arrest, July 18, 1831," The Cherokee Collection, acc. no. 1787, microfilm no. 815, Tennessee State Library and Archives.

20. Wilkins, *Cherokee Tragedy*, 235-36; Perdue and Green, *Cherokee Removal*, 60.

21. Wilkins, *Cherokee Tragedy*, 236-37; Edward Everett Dale and Gaston Litton, *Cherokee Cavaliers*, 1939 (reprint, Norman and London: University of Oklahoma Press, 1995), 8; Perdue and Green, *Cherokee Removal*, 60.

22. Wilkins, *Cherokee Tragedy*, 235-40.

23. Ibid., 206-7.
24. Elias Boudinot, *Cherokee Phoenix and Indians' Advocate*, 11 Aug. 1832: 2; Wilkins, *Cherokee Tragedy*, 244-45; Elias Boudinot, *Cherokee Editor: The Writings of Elias Boudinot*, Theda Perdue, ed., 1983 (Athens and London: University of Georgia Press, 1996), 25-26; Gary E. Moulton, *John Ross: Cherokee Chief* (Athens: University of Georgia Press, 1978), 65.
25. Wilkins, *Cherokee Tragedy*, 261; Charles C. Royce, "The Cherokee Nation of Indians: A Narrative of Their Official Relations with the Colonial and Federal Governments," *Fifth Annual Report of the Bureau of Ethnology to the Secretary of the Smithsonian Institution* (Washington, D.C.: Government Printing Office, 1887), 275.
26. Wilkins, *Cherokee Tragedy*, 266.
27. Ibid., 280-81.
28. Bass, *Cherokee Messenger*, 174; Moulton, *John Ross*, 69; John Howard Payne, "The Cherokee Cause," *Journal of Cherokee Studies* 1 (Summer 1976): 17.
29. Bass, *Cherokee Messenger*, 171; Thornton, "The Demography of the Trail of Tears Period," 78; Wilkins, *Cherokee Tragedy*, 285-89, 291-92; John R. Finger, "The Impact of Removal on the North Carolina Cherokees," *Cherokee Removal: Before and After*, William L. Anderson, ed. (Athens and London: University of Georgia Press, 1991), 96; Douglas C. Wilms, "Cherokee Land Use in Georgia Before Removal," *Cherokee Removal: Before and After*, William L. Anderson, ed. (Athens and London: University of Georgia Press, 1991), 18.
30. Finger, "Impact," 96, 98; Royce, "The Cherokee Nation of Indians," 284-85.
31. Wilms, "Cherokee Land Use," 18.
32. Wilkins, *Cherokee Tragedy*, 295.
33. Bass, *Cherokee Messenger*, 171; Royce, "The Cherokee Nation of Indians," 286.

34. Grant Foreman, *Indian Removal: The Emigration of the Five Civilized Tribes of Indians*, 1932 (2d ed., Norman: University of Oklahoma Press, 1953), 269; William M. Davis to the secretary of war, March 5, 1836, printed in Royce, "The Cherokee Nation of Indians," 284-85.

35. Thornton, "The Demography of the Trail of Tears Period," 87; Wilms, "Cherokee Land Use," 18.

36. Bill Jones, "Detachments of Emigrating Cherokee," *Trail of Tears Association Tennessee Chapter Newsletter*, Jan.-Apr. 2001: 5-6.

37. Jones, "Detachments," 5; John Ehle, *Trail of Tears: The Rise and Fall of the Cherokee Nation*, 1988 (2d ed., New York: Anchor Books-Doubleday, 1989), 363-65.

38. Ehle, *Trail of Tears*, 366-67.

39. Ibid., 312, 318.

40. John R. Finger, *The Eastern Band of Cherokees: 1819-1900* (Knoxville: University of Tennessee Press, 1984), 18-19.

41. Winfield Scott, "Removal Order No. 34," May 24, 1838, *Journal of Cherokee Studies* 3 (Summer 1978): 147.

42. Zella Armstrong, *The History of Hamilton County and Chattanooga, Tennessee*, vol. 1 (Chattanooga: Lookout Publishing Company), 186.

43. Winfield Scott, "Orders No. 25," Cherokee Agency, Tennessee, May 17, 1838, National Archives and Records Administration, Bureau of Indian Affairs, RG 75, microfilm no.115.

44. James Mooney, "Myths of the Cherokee," *Nineteenth Annual Report of the Bureau of American Ethnology* (Washington, D.C.: Government Printing Office, 1900), 130.

45. William Jasper Cotter, *My Autobiography: By William Jasper Cotter, A.M.* (Nashville, Dallas, Richmond: Publishing House of the Methodist Episcopal Church South, 1917), 39-40.

46. Thornton, "The Demography of the Trail of Tears Period," 80; Scott, "Removal Order No. 34."

47. Vicki Rozema, *Footsteps of the Cherokees: A Guide to the Eastern Homelands of the Cherokee Nation* (Winston-Salem, N.C.: John F. Blair, Publisher, 1995), 248; Lieutenant E. D. Keyes map of General Scott's operations, *Trail of Tears National Historic Trail: Comprehensive Management and Use Plan, Map Supplement* (Denver, Colo.: Denver Service Center, U.S. Department of the Interior, National Park Service, 1992).

48. Lenoir Papers, Special Collections Library, University of Tennessee, Knoxville.

49. Nathaniel Smith to C. A. Harris, Cherokee Agency East, June 1, 1838, NARA, BIA, RG 75, microfilm no. 115.

50. General Winfield Scott to Nathaniel Smith, Cherokee Agency, June 6, 1838, NARA, BIA, RG 75, microfilm no. 115.

51. Edward Deas, *Journal of Occurrences on the route of a party of Cherokee emigrants by Lt. E. Deas*, June 1838, NARA, BIA, RG 75, special file 249.

52. Winfield Scott to J. R. Poinsett, Cherokee Agency, Sept. 11, 1838, NARA, BIA, RG 75, microfilm no. 115; Winfield Scott to J. R. Poinsett, Cherokee Agency, July 19, 1838, NARA, BIA, RG 75, microfilm no. 115; Winfield Scott to Brigadier General Eustis, Cherokee Agency, June 24, 1838, NARA, BIA, RG 75, microfilm no. 115; Winfield Scott to General Jones, Cherokee Agency, July 17, 1838, NARA, BIA, RG 75, microfilm no. 115.

53. Winfield Scott to J. R. Poinsett, Cherokee Agency, June 26, 1838, NARA, BIA, RG 75, microfilm no. 115; Winfield Scott to J. R. Poinsett, Cherokee Agency, July 13, 1838, NARA, BIA, RG 75, microfilm no. 115.

54. General Winfield Scott to Joel R. Poinsett, Cherokee Agency, June 26, 1838, NARA, BIA, RG 75, microfilm no. 115.

55. R. H. K. Whitely, "Journal of Occurrences," printed in Duane King, "At the Point of a Bayonet: The Military Removal of Three Detachments of Georgia Cherokees in June 1838," unpublished manuscript, 1993, 12-17; G. S. Drane to Winfield Scott, Cherokee Agency, Oct. 17, 1838, NARA, BIA, RG 75, microfilm no. 115.

56. Winfield Scott to J. R. Poinsett, Cherokee Agency, June 18, 1838, NARA, BIA, RG 75, microfilm no. 115; Winfield Scott to G. Lowery and other Cherokee leaders, Cherokee Agency, June 19, 1838, NARA, BIA, RG 75, microfilm no. 115.

57. L. B. Webster to Frances, June 28, 1838, from "Letters from a Lonely Soldier," *Journal of Cherokee Studies* 3 (Summer 1978): 154.

58. General Winfield Scott, "Order No. 62," Cherokee Agency, NARA, BIA, RG 75, microfilm no. 115.

59. Arrell M. Gibson, *The Chickasaws* (Norman: University of Oklahoma Press, 1971), 193.

60. *Missionary Herald*, Dec. 1838.

61. Winfield Scott to J. R. Poinsett, Cherokee Agency, July 27, 1838, NARA, BIA, RG 75, microfilm no. 115; Winfield Scott to Brigadier General Jones, Cherokee Agency, July 23, 1838, NARA, BIA, RG 75, microfilm no. 115.

62. Jones, "Detachments," 5-6; Jones, "Drew Detachment"; Scott, "Order No. 62"; Deas, *Journal of Occurrences*, Apr. 1838, NARA, BIA, RG 75, special file 249.

63. John Ross, *The Papers of Chief John Ross*, Gary E. Moulton, ed., vol. 1 (Norman: University of Oklahoma Press, 1985), 42-53.

64. Foreman, *Indian Removal*, 302-3 n18.

65. H. B. Henegar, "Recollections of Cherokee Removal," 1897, reprinted in *Journal of Cherokee Studies* 3 (Summer 1978): 177.

66. Jones, "Detachments," 5-6; Bill Jones, "The John Drew Detachment," *Trail of Tears Association Tennessee Chapter Newsletter* (Nov.-Dec. 2000): 2; Daniel Sabin Butrick, *The Journal of Daniel Sabin Butrick: 1819-1845*, microfilm located at New Echota State Park, original ABC 18.3.3 vol. 4, American Board of Commissioners for Foreign Missions archives, by permission of Houghton Library, Harvard University, and Wider Church Ministries of the United Church of Christ, successor of the American Board of Commissioners for Foreign Missions; Deas, *Journal of Occurrences*, Apr. 1838; Deas, *Journal of Occurences*, June 1838; *Trail of Tears National Historic Trail: Comprehensive Management and Use Plan* (Denver, Colo.: Denver Service Center, U.S. Department of the Interior, National Park Service, 1992); *Trail of Tears NHT: Comprehensive Plan, Map Supplement.*

67. Martin Davis to Daniel Davis, Dec. 26, 1838, reprinted in Mattie Lorraine Adams, *The Family Tree of Daniel and Rachel Davis* (Duluth, Ga.: Claxton Printing Co., 1973), 24.

68. "Native of Maine, Traveling in the Western Country," originally printed in *New York Observer*, 16 Jan. 1839, reprinted in *Journal of Cherokee Studies* 3 (Summer 1978): 174-75.

69. Foreman, *Indian Removal*, 303; Joan Gilbert, *The Trail of Tears across Missouri* (Columbia and London: University of Missouri Press, 1996), 40, 45; Perdue, "The Conflict Within," 60-61.

70. Gilbert, *Trail of Tears*, 58-59, 90-91.

71. Jones, "The John Drew Detachment," 2; John Ross to William B. Lewis, financial account and explanation of the water detachments during Cherokee emigration, National Archives and Records Administration, Old Military and Civil Records, NWCTB-217-2AUDAIE525-6289A.

72. Jones, "Detachments," 6; Ross to Lewis, "Financial Account"; Jones, "The John Drew Detachment," 2.

73. Winfield Scott, requisition for funds, Athens, Tenn., Nov. 9, 1838, Cherokee Collection, acc. no. 1787, microfilm no. 815, Tennessee State Library and Archives.

74. Foreman, *Indian Removal*, 160, 311; Arthur H. DeRosier Jr., *The Removal of the Choctaw Indians*, 1970 (2d printing, Knoxville: University of Tennessee Press, 1972), 130, 137, 147, 157; Brad Agnew, *Fort Gibson: Terminal on the Trail of Tears*, 1980 (reprint, Norman and London: University of Oklahoma Press, 1989), 92; Nathaniel Smith to C. A. Harris, Feb. 28, 1838, NARA, BIA, RG 75, microfilm no. 115; John Ridge to J. Van Horn, Park Hill, Feb. 22, 1838, NARA, BIA, RG 75, microfilm no. 115; J. R. Stephenson to C. A. Harris, Fort Gibson, Aug. 28, 1838, NARA, BIA, RG 75, microfilm no. 115.

75. Wilkins, *Cherokee Tragedy*, 330-41; Grant Foreman, *The Five Civilized Tribes: Cherokee, Chickasaw, Choctaw, Creek, Seminole* (Norman: University of Oklahoma Press, 1934), 291-95; *Niles National Register*, 5 Oct. 1839, 85.

76. Mooney, "Myths of the Cherokee," 174-75.

77. Foreman, *The Five Civilized Tribes*, 282-83.

78. Perdue and Green, *The Cherokee Removal*, 170-73.

79. Thornton, "The Demography of the Trail of Tears Period," 80; Finger, "Impact," 103.

80. Thornton, "The Demography of the Trail of Tears Period," 93; King, "At the Point of a Bayonet," 20-21.

81. Conversation with Hastings Shade, Deputy Chief of the Cherokee Nation of Oklahoma, October 17, 2002, Trail of Tears Conference, Ft. Smith, Ark.

82. Ibid., 75, 85.

I Hope My Bones Will Not Be Deserted by You

1. Wilkins, *Cherokee Tragedy*, 208.

2. *Cherokee Phoenix and Indians' Advocate*, 3 Apr. 1828: 1.

3. *Cherokee Phoenix and Indians' Advocate*, 28 Oct. 1829: 3.

First Blood Shed by the Georgians

1. Wilkins, *Cherokee Tragedy*, 210; *Cherokee Phoenix*, 9 Sept. 1829-26 March 1831; Boudinot, *Cherokee Editor*, 149 n47, 149-50 n49; Moulton, *John Ross*, 40.
2. *Cherokee Phoenix*, 9 Sept. 1829–26 March 1831; Moulton, *John Ross*, 40.
3. Moulton, *John Ross*, 40; Ehle, *Trail of Tears*, 225-26; Wilkins, *Cherokee Tragedy*, 211-12.
4. Ehle, *Trail of Tears*, 227.
5. Ehle, *Trail of Tears*, 226; Wilkins, *Cherokee Tragedy*, 212.
6. *Cherokee Phoenix and Indians' Advocate*, 9 Sept. 1829, 10 Feb. 1830, 7 Apr. 1830, 26 March 1831.
7. Elias Boudinot, "First Blood Shed by the Georgians," *Cherokee Phoenix and Indians' Advocate*, 10 Feb.1830: 2.

The Enemies of Georgia

1. Bass, *Cherokee Messenger*, 3, 4, 78.
2. Ibid., 129.
3. William G. McLoughlin, *Cherokees and Missionaries, 1789-1839*, 1984 (reprint, Norman and London: University of Oklahoma Press, 1995), 256, 291.
4. McLoughlin, *Cherokees and Missionaries*, 257-58; Wilkins, *Cherokee Tragedy*, 225-26.
5. McLoughlin, *Cherokees and Missionaries*, 257-58; Wilkins, *Cherokee Tragedy*, 225-26; Bass, *Cherokee Messenger*, 130.
6. McLoughlin, *Cherokees and Missionaries*, 261.
7. Bass, *Cherokee Messenger*, 130-32.
8. McLoughlin, *Cherokees and Missionaries*, 262, 295.
9. McLoughlin, *Cherokees and Missionaries*, 262; Bass, *Cherokee Messenger*, 137.
10. Bass, *Cherokee Messenger*, 137.
11. Bass, *Cherokee Messenger*, 142; Wilkins, *Cherokee Tragedy*, 227; Worcester, "Mr. Worcester's Account of His Second Arrest."

12. Bass, *Cherokee Messenger*, 147.
13. Bass, *Cherokee Messenger*, 139, 154-55; *Cherokee Phoenix and Indians' Advocate*, 26 March 1831: 3; 16 Apr. 1831: 3; McLoughlin, *Cherokees and Missionaries*, 262-64.
14. Bass, *Cherokee Messenger*, 5, 159; McLoughlin, *Cherokees and Missionaries*, 264-65.
15. Bass, *Cherokee Messenger*, 5, 175-76.
16. *Missionary Herald*, Jan. 1837.
17. Worcester, "Mr. Worcester's Account of His Second Arrest."

That Paper Called a Treaty

1. Royce, "The Cherokee Nation of Indians," 284.
2. Ibid., 284-85.

Your Fate Is Decided

1. Ehle, *Trail of Tears*, 226; Wilkins, *Cherokee Tragedy*, 295; McLoughlin, *Cherokees and Missionaries*, 322.
2. Ehle, *Trail of Tears*, 300-301; McLoughlin, *Cherokees and Missionaries*, 322-23.
3. Moulton, *John Ross*, 79; Wilkins, *Cherokee Tragedy*, 296-97.
4. Moulton, *John Ross*, 308; Wilkins, *Cherokee Tragedy*, 298-99.
5. *American State Papers: Military Affairs* (Washington, D.C.: Gales and Seaton, 1861), 7: 566.
6. Wilkins, *Cherokee Tragedy*, 316; Moulton, *John Ross*, 79; Ehle, *Trail of Tears*, 302.
7. Moulton, *John Ross*, 79, 83; Ehle, *Trail of Tears*, 309-10.
8. John E. Wool, "Appeal to the Cherokees—March 22, 1837," Cherokee Collection, acc. no. 1787, microfilm no. 815, Tennessee State Library and Archives.

The Talk

1. Moulton, *John Ross*, 82-83.
2. Moulton, *John Ross*, 84-85; Brian M. Butler, "The Red Clay Council Ground," *Journal of Cherokee Studies* 2 (Winter 1977): 142-45.
3. Moulton, *John Ross*, 85; George W. Featherstonhaugh, *A Canoe Voyage up the Minnay Sotor*, vol. 2 (London: Richard Bentley, 1847), 220-60.
4. Featherstonhaugh, *A Canoe Voyage*, 236-37.
5. Ibid., 240-46.

Too Sick to Travel

1. Armstrong, *The History of Hamilton County and Chattanooga, Tennessee*, 188-89.
2. Jones, "Detachments," 5-6; B. B. Cannon, "Journal of Occurrences, Oct. 13, 1837," NARA, BIA, RG 75, special file 249; military correspondence of 1837-38, NARA, BIA, RG 75, microfilm no. 115 and Indian Accounts, RG 217.
3. Gilbert, *Trail of Tears*, 59-60.
4. Jones, "Detachments," 5-6; Cannon, "Journal of Occurrences"; Dr. G. S. Townsend to C. A. Harris, Jan. 25, 1838, NARA, BIA, RG 75, microfilm no. 115.
5. Cannon, "Journal of Occurrences."

A Distance Short of 800 Miles

1. Cannon, "Journal of Occurrences"; Dr. G. S. Townsend to C. A. Harris, June 25, 1838, NARA, BIA, RG 75, microfilm no. 115.
2. Dr. G. S. Townsend to C. A. Harris, June 22, 1838, NARA, BIA, RG 75, microfilm no. 115.
3. Dr. G. S. Townsend to C. A. Harris, Jan. 25, 1838, NARA, BIA, RG 75, microfilm no. 115.
4. Ibid.

Under Weigh at Daylight

1. Scott, "Removal Order No. 34"; Jones, "Detachments," 5-6.
2. Deas, *Journal of Occurrences*, June 1838; Deas, *Journal of Occurrences*, Apr. 1838; Jones, "Detachments," 5-6.
3. Deas, *Journal of Occurrences*, June 1838; Brigadier General Charles Floyd, June 9, 1838, in King, "At the Point of a Bayonet"; Colonel William Lindsay to Winfield Scott, June 21, 1838, copy of letter from Shirley Lawrence of the Tennessee Trail of Tears Association.
4. Deas, *Journal of Occurrences*, June 1838.
5. Miscellaneous expense receipts in NARA, Indian Accounts, RG 217.
6. Lieutenant Edward Deas, "Memorandum to accompany disbursements" and other reports and vouchers in NARA, Indian Accounts, RG 217; Jones, "Detachments," 5-6.
7. Miscellaneous expense receipts for Lieutenant Edward Deas in NARA, Indian Accounts, RG 217.
8. Deas, *Journal of Occurrences*, June 1838.

Feelings of Discontent

1. Winfield Scott to J. R. Poinsett, Cherokee Agency, July 26, 1838, NARA, BIA, RG 75, microfilm no. 115.
2. Jones, "Detachments," 5-6; Whitely's journal in King, "At the Point of a Bayonet," 12-17.
3. Jones, "Detachments," 5-6; Ehle, *Trail of Tears*, 391; Nathaniel Smith to Winfield Scott, Cherokee Agency, Aug. 7, 1838, NARA, BIA, RG 75, microfilm no. 115; G. S. Drane to Winfield Scott, Cherokee Agency, Oct. 17, 1838, NARA, BIA, RG 75, microfilm no. 115.
4. Smith to Scott, Aug. 7, 1838.
5. Drane to Scott, Oct. 17, 1838.

Until the Sickly Season Should Pass Away

1. Colonel William Lindsay to Colonel W. J. Worth, Chatta-nooga, June 18, 1838, copy of letter from Shirley Lawrence of the Tennessee Trail of Tears Association.
2. Winfield Scott to J. R. Poinsett, July 27, 1838, NARA, BIA, RG 75, microfilm no. 115; Foreman, *Indian Removal*, 187.
3. Winfield Scott to Brigadier General Eustis, June 19, 1838, Cherokee Agency, NARA, BIA, RG 75, microfilm no. 115; Winfield Scott to G. Lowery and Cherokee leaders, June 19, 1838, Cherokee Agency, NARA, BIA, RG 75, microfilm no. 115; Winfield Scott to J. R. Poinsett, July 24, 1838, Cherokee Agency, NARA, BIA, RG 75, microfilm no. 115.
4. John Ross and the Cherokee Council to General Winfield Scott, July 23, 1838, NARA, BIA, RG 75, microfilm no. 115; Winfield Scott to John Ross and the Cherokee Council, July 25, 1838, NARA, BIA, RG 75, microfilm no. 115; resolution of the Cherokee Council, Aquohee Camps, July 28, 1838, NARA, BIA, RG 75, microfilm no. 115.
5. John Ross, "Accounts for Removal Detachment Expenses," Ross, *The Papers of Chief John Ross*, 2: 42-53.
6. Correspondence between John Adair Bell and Winfield Scott and Winfield Scott to Lieutenant Edward Deas, 1838, NARA, BIA, RG 75, microfilm no. 115.
7. John Ross and the Cherokee Council to General Winfield Scott, July 23, 1838.
8. Winfield Scott to John Ross and the Cherokee Council, July 25, 1838.
9. Resolution of the Cherokee Council, Aquohee Camps, July 28.

For the Comfort and Well-being of This People

1. "Map of Fort Cass," *Trail of Tears NHT: Comprehensive Plan, Map Supplement.*
2. Henry Martin Wiltse, "History of Chattanooga," unpublished manuscript, acc. no. 92, Chattanooga-Hamilton County Bicentennial Library.
3. Colonel William Lindsay to General Winfield Scott, June 21, 1838.
4. Dr. John S. Young to Nathaniel Smith, Aug. 19, 1838, NARA, BIA, RG 75, microfilm no. 115.
5. Colonel William Laus to Captain Robert Anderson, Missionary Hill, Aug. 19, 1838, copy from Shirley Lawrence of the Tennessee Trail of Tears Association.
6. Captain John Page to C. A. Harris, July 25, 1838, Calhoun, Tenn., NARA, BIA, RG 75, microfilm no. 115.
7. Dr. J. W. Lide to Captain John Page, July 25, 1838, Cherokee Agency, NARA, BIA, RG 75, microfilm no. 115.

The Sadness of the Heart

1. Starr, Emmet, *History of the Cherokee Indians and Their Legends and Folk Lore,* 1922 (reprint, Millwood, N.Y.: Kraus Reprint Co., 1977), 103; *Journal of Cherokee Studies* 3 (Summer 1978): 187; Jones, "Detachments," 5; Winfield Scott to J. R. Poinsett, Aug. 31, 1838, Headquarters Eastern Division Cherokee Agency, NARA, BIA, RG 75, microfilm no. 115.
2. Winfield Scott to J. R. Poinsett, Aug. 31, 1838.
3. John Page to C. A. Harris, Sept. 4, 1838, Calhoun, Tenn., NARA, BIA, RG 75, microfilm no. 115.
4. John Ross, "Accounts for Removal Detachment Expenses," 2: 43.

5. Lieutenant H. L. Scott to General Winfield Scott, Oct. 11, 1838, Fort Cass, Tenn., NARA, BIA, RG 75, microfilm no. 115.

6. Foreman, *Removal*, 232, 241, 247; Bass, *Cherokee Messenger*, 971.

7. John Howard Payne, "The Cherokee Cause," *Journal of Cherokee Studies* 1 (Summer 1976): 17; Wilkins, *Cherokee Tragedy*, 278-84; Boudinot, *Cherokee Editor*, 206-7, 226 n5.

8. William Shorey Coodey to John Howard Payne, Washington City, Aug. 13, 1840, Papers of John Howard Payne, MS 689, Edward E. Ayer Collection, Newberry Library, Chicago.

A Year of Spiritual Darkness

1. Wilkins, *Cherokee Tragedy*, 119, 226; *Missionary Herald*, Jan. 1837.

2. Wilkins, *Cherokee Tragedy*, 226-27; McLoughlin, *Cherokees and Missionaries*, 256.

3. Butrick, *Journal*, May 26–Oct. 31, 1838.

4. Jones, "Detachments," 5-6; Foreman, *Indian Removal*, 311; Butrick, *Journal*, Oct. 2, 1838, Nov. 1, 1838; "Emigration Detachments," *Journal of Cherokee Studies* 3 (Summer 1978): 187.

5. Jones, "Detachments," 5-6; Butrick, *Journal*, May 26, 1838, June 17, 1838; "Emigration of Detachments," 187.

6. Butrick, *Journal*, June 10-17, 1838; Dec. 18-31, 1838.

Hail, Rain, Wind and Thunder

1. Butrick, *Journal*, Sabbath (Sept. 9), Thurs., Oct. 2; Dr. J. W. Lide to Captain John Page, July 25, 1838, Cherokee Agency, NARA, BIA, RG 75, microfilm no. 115; Dr. J. J. Morrow, "Journal," printed in Wiltse, *History of Chattanooga*, 77-79; "Emigration Detachments," 187.
2. Dr. J. J. Morrow, "Journal," printed in Wiltse, *History of Chattanooga*, 77-79; Butrick, *Journal*.
3. Dr. J. J. Morrow, "Journal," printed in Wiltse, *History of Chattanooga*, 77-79.
4. Ibid., 77-79.

One Old Man Named T*sali*

1. John R. Finger, *The Eastern Band of Cherokees: 1819-1900*, 22-25; John R. Finger, "The Saga of Tsali: Legend Versus Reality," *North Carolina Historical Review* 56:12; Duane King and E. Raymond Evans, "Tsali: The Man Behind the Legend," *Journal of Cherokee Studies* 4 (Fall 1979): 194-201.
2. Henry Prince, *Amidst a Storm of Bullets: The Diary of Lt. Henry Prince in Florida: 1836-1842*, Frank Laumer, ed. (Tampa, Fla.: University of Tampa Press: 1998), 127; Finger, *The Eastern Band*, 25-26; Mooney, "Myths of the Cherokee," 157-58.
3. Finger, *The Eastern Band*, 3, 27.
4. Finger, *The Eastern Band*, 24-28.
5. Mooney, "Myths of the Cherokee," 131, 157-58.
6. Lieutenant C. H. Larned to Winfield Scott, Fort Cass, Nov. 5, 1838, NARA, BIA, RG 75, microfilm no. 115; John Page to T. Hartley Crawford, Calhoun, Tenn., Dec. 4, 1838, NARA, BIA, RG 75, microfilm no. 115; Finger, "The Saga of Tsali," 7.
7. Mooney, "Myths of the Cherokee," 131.
8. Mooney, "Myths of the Cherokee," 157-58.

9. Lieutenant C. H. Larned to Winfield Scott, Fort Cass, Nov. 5, 1838.

10. John Page to T. Hartley Crawford, Calhoun, Tenn., Dec. 4, 1838.

Murdered from an Ambush

1. Jones, "Detachments," 6; Foreman, *The Five Civilized Tribes*, 292; Wilkins, *Cherokee Tragedy*, 330.

2. Foreman, *The Five Civilized Tribes*, 291-92; Wilkins, *Cherokee Tragedy*, 330-33.

3. Foreman, *The Five Civilized Tribes*, 292; Wilkins, *Cherokee Tragedy*, 333.

4. Wilkins, *Cherokee Tragedy*, 333-35.

5. *Niles' National Register*, 3 Aug. 1839, 362, 5 Oct. 1839, 85; Foreman, *The Five Civilized Tribes*, 292-93; Wilkins, *Cherokee Tragedy*, 335-36.

6. Foreman, *The Five Civilized Tribes*, 293; Wilkins, *Cherokee Tragedy*, 336-38.

7. Foreman, *The Five Civilized Tribes*, 293; Wilkins, *Cherokee Tragedy*, 338-39.

8. John Ross to Matthew Arbuckle, June 22, 1839, *The Papers of Chief John Ross*, 1: 717; Foreman, *The Five Civilized Tribes*, 294-95; Wilkins, *Cherokee Tragedy*, 340-41.

9. John Adair Bell and Stand Watie to *Arkansas Gazette*, reprinted in *Niles' National Register*, 5 Oct. 1839, 85; Wilkins, *Cherokee Tragedy*, 341.

10. Bell and Watie to *Arkansas Gazette*; Ross to Arbuckle, June 22, 1839, *The Papers of Chief John Ross*.

11. Bell and Watie to *Arkansas Gazette*.

12. Ross to Arbuckle, June 22, 1839, *The Papers of Chief John Ross*.

A Citizen of the State of North Carolina

1. William Holland Thomas, "Remarks of Mr. Thomas," *Weekly Standard* (Raleigh, N.C.), Dec. 8, 1858; Mooney, "Myths of the Cherokee," 164-65.
2. Lieutenant H. L. Scott to General Winfield Scott, Oct. 26, 1838, Fort Cass, NARA, BIA, RG 75, microfilm no. 115.
3. Winfield Scott to Colonel W. S. Foster, Athens, Tenn., Nov. 15, 1838, NARA, BIA, RG 75, microfilm no. 115; General Winfield Scott to J. R. Poinsett, Nov. 13, 1838, NARA, BIA, RG 75, microfilm no. 115; General Winfield Scott to Captain John Page, Nov. 15, 1838, Athens, Tenn., NARA, BIA, RG 75, microfilm no. 115; Prince, *Amidst a Storm of Bullets*, 128-32.
4. Mooney, "Myths of the Cherokee," 164-65.
5. Finger, "Impact," 106-7; Mooney, "Myths of the Cherokee," 164-65.
6. E. Stanley Godbold, Jr., and Mattie U. Russell, *Confederate Colonel and Cherokee Chief: The Life of William Holland Thomas* (Knoxville: University of Tennessee Press, 1990), 2, 9, 10-13, 85-86.
7. "Act in Favor of the Cherokee Chief Junoluskee," *Acts of the Assembly of North Carolina* (Raleigh), 128, Jan. 2, 1847.
8. Thomas, "Remarks of Mr. Thomas."

If Not Rejoicing, at Least in Comfort

1. Winfield Scott, *Memoirs of Lieut.-General Scott, LL.D.: Written by Himself*, vol. 1 (New York: Sheldon and Co., Publishers, 1864), 43, 117, 175, 217, 250-56, 628-29.
2. Ibid., 302.
3. Winfield Scott to J. R. Poinsett, Cherokee Agency, July 27, 1838, NARA, BIA, RG 75, microfilm no. 115.
4. Scott, *Memoirs*, 176.
5. Ibid., 317-29.

Appendix 1:
Guide to Cherokee Detachments, 1837-39

1.   John Ross, *The Papers of Chief John Ross*, 2: 42-53; Prince,
     Amidst a Storm of Bullets, 128-32; Foreman, *Indian Removal*,
     305, 309, 310-12; Jones, "Detachments," 5; "Emigration
     Detachments," 186-87; Lieutenant Whitely's Journal in
     King, "At the Point of a Bayonet," 12-17; Deas, *Journal of
     Occurrences*, June 1838; Deas, *Journal of Occurrences*, Apr.
     1838; Dr. C. Lillybridge to C. A. Harris, May 24, 1838,
     NARA, BIA, RG 75, microfilm no. 115; General Winfield
     Scott and Nathaniel Smith, NARA, BIA, RG 75, microfilm
     no. 115; Captain G. S. Drane to General Winfield Scott,
     Oct. 17, 1838, NARA, BIA, RG 75, microfilm no. 115.

Appendix 2:
General Winfield Scott's Removal Order No. 25

1.   Winfield Scott, "Orders. No. 25," Cherokee Agency,
     May 17, 1838, NARA, BIA, RG 75, microfilm no.115.

Appendix 3:
General Winfield Scott's Removal Order No. 62

1.   Winfield Scott, "Orders No. 62," Cherokee Agency, July 5,
     1838, NARA, BIA, RG 75, microfilm no.115.

Appendix 4:
General Winfield Scott's Circular to Cherokee Conductors

1.   Winfield Scott, "Circular Addressed to Cherokee Conduc-
     tors," Cherokee Agency, Oct. 4, 1838, NARA, BIA, RG 75,
     microfilm no.115.

Appendix 5:
General John E. Wool's General Order No. 74

1. John E. Wool, "General Order No. 74," Fort Cass, Tenn., Nov. 3, 1836, Cherokee Collection, acc. no. 1787, microfilm no. 815, Tennessee State Library and Archives.

BIBLIOGRAPHY

Adams, Mattie Lorraine. *The Family Tree of Daniel and Rachel Davis*. Duluth, Ga.: Claxton Printing Co., 1973.

Agnew, Brad. *Fort Gibson: Terminal on the Trail of Tears*. 1980. Reprint, Norman and London: University of Oklahoma Press, 1989.

American Board of Commissioners for Foreign Missions Archives. Houghton Library, Harvard University.

American State Papers: Class II, Indian Affairs. Vol. 1. Washington, D.C.: Gales and Seaton, 1832.

American State Papers: Military Affairs. Vol. 7. Washington, D.C.: Gales and Seaton, 1861.

Anderson, William L., ed. *Cherokee Removal: Before and After*. Athens and London: University of Georgia Press, 1991.

Armstrong, Zella. *The History of Hamilton County and Chattanooga, Tennessee*. Vol. 1. Chattanooga: Lookout Publishing Co.

Bass, Althea. *Cherokee Messenger*. 1936. Reprint, Norman and London: University of Oklahoma Press, 1996.

Boudinot, Elias. *Cherokee Editor: The Writings of Elias Boudinot*. Edited by Theda Perdue. 1983. Reprint, Athens and London: University of Georgia Press, 1996.

Butler, Brian M. "The Red Clay Council Ground." *Journal of Cherokee Studies* 2 (Winter 1977): 140-52.

Cherokee Collection, The. Tennessee State Library and Archives, Nashville.

Cherokee Phoenix and Indians' Advocate, 6 March 1828-10 February 1830.

Cotter, William Jasper. *My Autobiography: By William Jasper Cotter, A.M.* Nashville, Dallas, and Richmond: Publishing House of the Methodist Episcopal Church South, 1917.

Dale, Edward Everett, and Gaston Litton. *Cherokee Cavaliers.* 1939. Reprint, Norman and London: University of Oklahoma Press, 1995.

DeRosier, Arthur H., Jr. *The Removal of the Choctaw Indians.* 1970. 2d printing, Knoxville: University of Tennessee Press, 1972.

Ehle, John. *Trail of Tears: The Rise and Fall of the Cherokee Nation.* 1988. 2d ed., New York: Anchor Books-Doubleday, 1989.

Evarts, Jeremiah. *Cherokee Removal: The William Penn Essays and Other Writings.* Edited and with an introduction by Francis Paul Prucha. Knoxville: University of Tennessee Press, 1981.

Featherstonhaugh, George W. *A Canoe Voyage up the Minnay Sotor.* Vol. 2. London: Richard Bentley, 1847.

Filler, Louis, and Allen Guttmann, eds. *The Removal of the Cherokee Nation: Manifest Destiny or National Dishonor?* Huntington, N.Y.: Robert E. Krieger Publishing Co., 1977.

Finger, John R. *The Eastern Band of Cherokees: 1819-1900.* Knoxville: University of Tennessee Press, 1984.

———. "The Saga of Tsali: Legend Versus Reality." *North Carolina Historical Review* 56: 1-18.

Foreman, Grant. *The Five Civilized Tribes: Cherokee, Chickasaw, Choctaw, Creek, Seminole.* Norman: University of Oklahoma Press, 1934.

———. *Indian Removal: The Emigration of the Five Civilized Tribes of Indians.* 1932. 2d ed., Norman: University of Oklahoma Press, 1953.

Gibson, Arrell M. *The Chickasaws.* Norman: University of Oklahoma Press, 1971.

Gilbert, Joan. *The Trail of Tears across Missouri.* Columbia and London: University of Missouri Press, 1996.

Godbold, E. Stanley, Jr., and Mattie U. Russell. *Confederate Colonel and Cherokee Chief: The Life of William Holland Thomas*. Knoxville: University of Tennessee Press, 1990.

Henegar, H. B. "Recollections of Cherokee Removal." 1897. Reprinted in *Journal of Cherokee Studies* 3 (Summer 1978): 177-79.

Horsman, Reginald. *Expansion and American Indian Policy, 1783-1812*. 1967. Reprint, Norman and London: University of Oklahoma Press, 1992.

Jones, Bill. "Deserters along the Trail of Tears." *Trail of Tears Association Tennessee Chapter Newsletter* (August-October 2000): 2.

———. "Detachments of Emigrating Cherokees." *Trail of Tears Association Tennessee Chapter Newsletter* (January-April 2001): 5-6.

———. "The John Drew Detachment." *Trail of Tears Association Tennessee Chapter Newsletter* (November-December 2000): 2.

King, Duane. "At the Point of a Bayonet: The Military Removal of Three Detachments of Georgia Cherokees in June 1838." Unpublished manuscript, 1993. Obtained from the Tennessee Trail of Tears Association.

King, Duane, and E. Raymond Evans. "Tsali: The Man Behind the Legend." *Journal of Cherokee Studies* 4 (Fall 1979): 194-201.

Lenoir Papers. Special Collections Library, University of Tennessee, Knoxville.

McLoughlin, William G. *After the Trail of Tears: The Cherokees' Struggle for Sovereignty, 1839-1880*. Chapel Hill: University of North Carolina Press, 1993.

———. *Cherokees and Missionaries, 1789-1839*. 1984. Reprint, Norman and London: University of Oklahoma Press, 1995.

Missionary Herald, January 1837–December 1838.

Mooney, James. "Myths of the Cherokee." *Nineteenth Annual Report of the Bureau of American Ethnology*. Washington, D.C.: Government Printing Office, 1900.

Moulton, Gary E. *John Ross: Cherokee Chief*. Athens: University of Georgia Press, 1978.

National Archives and Records Administration, Bureau of Indian Affairs. Indian Records and Old Military and Civil Records.

"Native of Maine, Traveling in the Western Country, A." Originally printed in the *New York Observer*, 16 January 1839. Reprint, *Journal of Cherokee Studies* 3 (Summer 1978): 174-75.

Niles' National Register, 17 August 1839–5 October 1839. Special Collections Library, University of Tennessee, Knoxville.

North Carolina General Assembly. *Acts of the Assembly of North Carolina*. Raleigh, 2 January 1847.

Payne, John Howard. "The Cherokee Cause." *Journal of Cherokee Studies* 1 (Summer 1976): 17-22.

———. Papers. Edward E. Ayer Collection, Newberry Library, Chicago.

Perdue, Theda, and Michael D. Green, eds. *The Cherokee Removal: A Brief History with Documents*. With an introduction by the editors. Boston and New York: Bedford Books of St. Martin's Press, 1995.

Prince, Henry. *Amidst a Storm of Bullets: The Diary of Lt. Henry Prince in Florida: 1836-1842*. Edited by Frank Laumer. Tampa, Fla.: University of Tampa Press: 1998.

Records of the Bureau of Indian Affairs. National Archives. Record Group 75.

Ross, John. *The Papers of Chief John Ross*. Edited by Gary E. Moulton. Norman: University of Oklahoma Press, 1985.

Royce, Charles C. "The Cherokee Nation of Indians: A Narrative of Their Official Relations with the Colonial and Federal Governments." *Fifth Annual Report of the Bureau of Ethnology to the Secretary of the Smithsonian Institution*. Washington, D.C.: Government Printing Office, 1887.

Rozema, Vicki. *Footsteps of the Cherokees: A Guide to the Eastern Homelands of the Cherokee Nation*. Winston-Salem, N.C.: John F. Blair, Publisher, 1995.

Satz, Ronald N. *American Indian Policy in the Jacksonian Era*. Lincoln: University of Nebraska Press, 1975.

Scott, Winfield. *Memoirs of Lieut.-General Scott, LL.D.: Written by Himself*. 2 vols. New York: Sheldon and Co., Publishers, 1864.

————. "Orders No. 34." *Journal of Cherokee Studies* 3 (Summer 1978): 147.

Speeches on the Passage of the Bill for the Removal of the Indians, Delivered in the Congress of the United States, April and May 1830. Boston: Perkins and Marvin; New York: Jonathan Leavitt, 1830.

Starr, Emmet. *History of the Cherokee Indians and Their Legends and Folk Lore*. 1921. Reprint, Millwood, N.Y.: Kraus Reprint Co., 1977.

Trail of Tears National Historic Trail: Comprehensive Management and Use Plan. Denver, Colo.: Denver Service Center, U.S. Department of the Interior, National Park Service, 1992.

Trail of Tears National Historic Trail: Comprehensive Management and Use Plan, Map Supplement. Denver, Colo.: Denver Service Center, U.S. Department of the Interior, National Park Service, 1992.

Walker, Robert Sparks. *Torchlights to the Cherokees: The Brainerd Mission*. New York: Macmillan, 1931.

Webster, L. B. "Letters from a Lonely Soldier." *Journal of Cherokee Studies* 3 (Summer 1978): 153-57.

Weekly Standard (Raleigh, N.C.), 8 December 1858.

Wilkins, Thurman. *Cherokee Tragedy: The Story of the Ridge Family and the Decimation of a People*. 1970. 2d ed., Norman and London: University of Oklahoma Press, 1986.

Wiltse, Henry Martin. "History of Chattanooga." Unpublished manuscript at the Chattanooga-Hamilton County Bicentennial Library.

INDEX